Fra Angelico

Silvia Malaguzzi

GIUNTI

FIRENZE MVSEI

Graphic design: Giovanni Breschi

Translation: Catherine Frost

Cover: *St Dominic*,
detail of the fresco with
The Mocking of Christ,
1438-1443. Florence,
San Marco Museum.

First edition: May 2003

www.giunti.it

ISBN 88-09-03054-0

Reprint	Year
6 5 4 3 2 1 0	2007 2006 2005 2004 2003

Printed by Giunti Industrie Grafiche S.p.A. – Prato - Italy

Contents

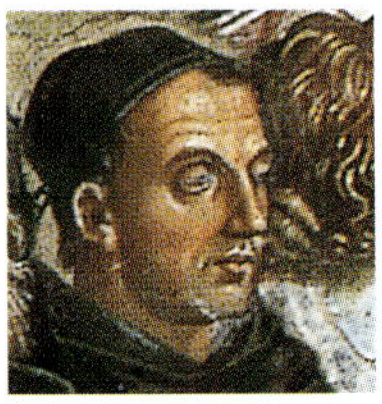

The apprenticeship years

«Angelicus pictor» was the term used in 1469 by Domenico di Giovanni da Corella, a friar in the order of the Observant Dominicans, in his *Theotokon*, in reference to his famous brother monk Giovanni, thus conferring on him the pseudonym under which he was to pass into history. Both pseudonym and definition, the adjective *angelicus* suggests that both his figurative talent as well as his inspiration had a "divine" origin, and that the nature of his spirit and his religious calling was a higher one.

Both Dominican friar and master painter, Fra Angelico, or Beato Angelico as he is also called, is a singular figure of artist-theologian whose complexity is accentuated by his significant dual role as innovator among the pioneers of Renaissance painting and highly cultured interpreter of 15th century religiosity, enriched by the values of Humanism. Starting in the third decade of the 15th century, in fact, he developed a personal response to the complex demands of his milieu, creating works of religious subject in which the didactic urge of a spirituality inspired by the most genuine Evangelical message blended with a personal figurative sensitivity that was highly attentive to recent innovations.

But who was Fra Angelico? In what atmosphere did his talent develop? What standards of excellence did his art, so mystic and at the same time so modern, strive to attain? Fra Giovanni, in the world Guido di Piero, was born near the town of Vicchio, in the Mugello region, near the end of the 14th century. Very little information exists on the family he came from, its members and their social standing. It is known that his brother Benedetto also chose the religious life, becoming a friar in the same Dominican monastery of San Domenico at Fiesole. Here the two brothers established a flourishing illuminators' school.

The unusual presence in the same family of two religious callings has suggested that in reality the brothers may have entered a monastery due to

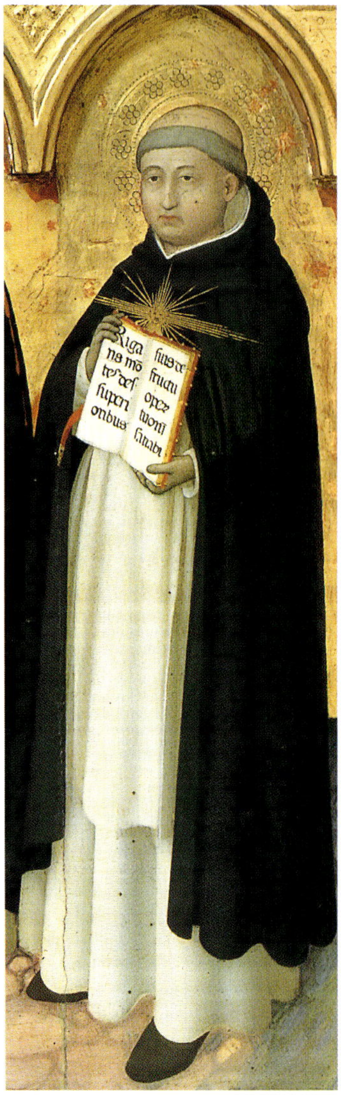

San Pietro Martire Triptych, detail of *Thomas Aquinas*, 1424-1425. Florence, San Marco Museum.

circumstances of extreme poverty rather than spiritual motivations. The lack of documentation on the family could represent an implicit confirmation of this hypothesis, although some traces exist of Fra Angelico's successful career prior to 1423, the year in which he was mentioned for the first time as "frate Giovanni de' frati di San Domenicho da Fiesole".

Giorgio Vasari, in his biography of Fra Angelico, notes that "Although he could have lived most comfortably in the secular world, and in addition to what he already owned, could have earned whatever he wanted from the arts in which, even as a young man, he was already proficient, he nevertheless desired, for his own satisfaction and tranquility, being by nature calm and gentle, and principally for the salvation of his soul, to join the Order of the Preaching Friars". If the words of Vasari, who wrote this passage in his *Lives* in 1568, inspired also by hagiographical intentions, cannot be considered the final word on the subject, it is true that documents exist in-

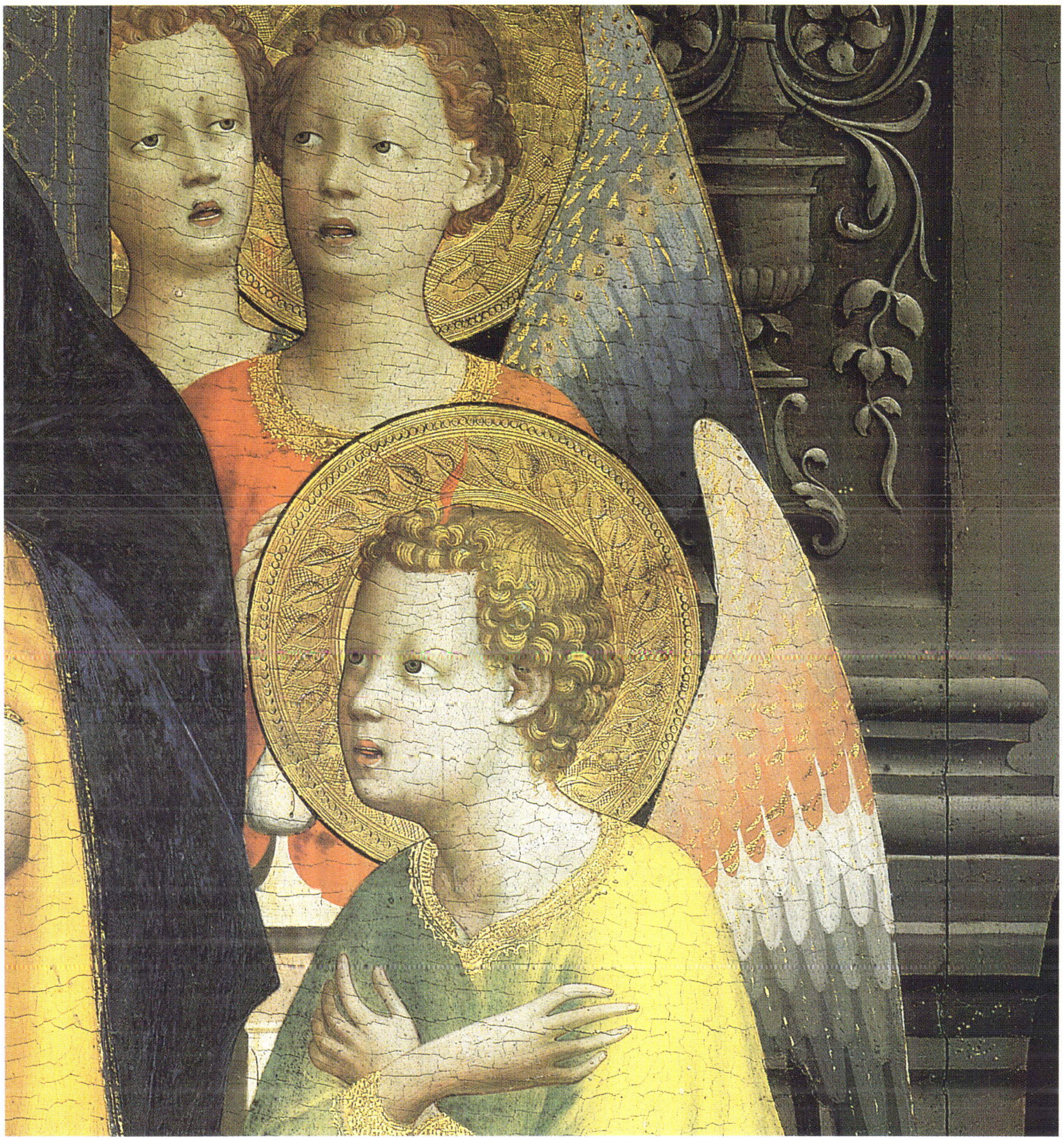

At right: *San Domenico Altarpiece*, detail, 1420-1424. Fiesole, San Domenico.

Angels, the messengers of God, appear very frequently in the works of Fra Angelico. The gowns they wear usually display vivid symbolic colors while their wings present the multi-color shading characteristic of the archaic tradition. A flame over the head of the praying angel (shown here) indicates that he is a seraphim and thus belongs to the angelic rank of spiritual beings entrusted with representing divine love visually.

Upper left: *Portrait of Fra Angelico*, detail of Luca Signorelli's fresco depicting the *Preaching of the Anti-Christ* in the San Brizio Chapel at Orvieto, 1499-1502.

dicating Fra Angelico's activity before he entered the Dominican order, documents which seem to provide implicit proof of his sincere vocation. The first mention of the painter dates back to 1417, the year in which he was documented as being a member of the Compagnia di San Niccolò del Carmine following his presentation by the well-known illuminator Battista di Biagio Sanguigni. By that date, then, Fra Angelico must have already achieved professional standing and was receiving the income deriving from his profession. Another document from 1418 certifies payment for an important commission: a panel painted for the Florentine church of Santo Stefano al Ponte Vecchio. On the basis of this information the hypothesis that he had become a friar due to financial need seems less probable; spiritual rather than material reasons must have motivated his decision.

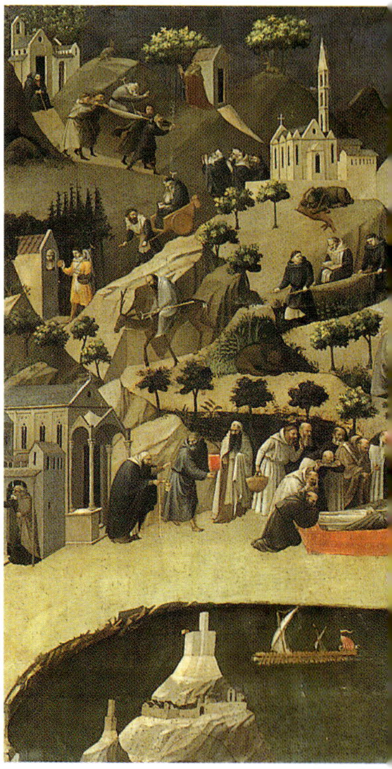

In 1423 Fra Angelico received payment for a now lost *Crucifix* painted for the Dominican church of Santa Maria Novella. In that year he was present for the first time in the monastery of San Domenico at Fiesole showing that, although he had entered the order only recently, he was allowed to pursue the career of a painter. The order would not have objected to this, seeing no conflict between the practice of art and correct monastic behavior. On this subject, a question arises, whether the case of Fra Angelico was a frequent one or whether it was instead an exception dictated by special consideration for the young monk's extraordinary talent, or perhaps by the needs of the order itself.

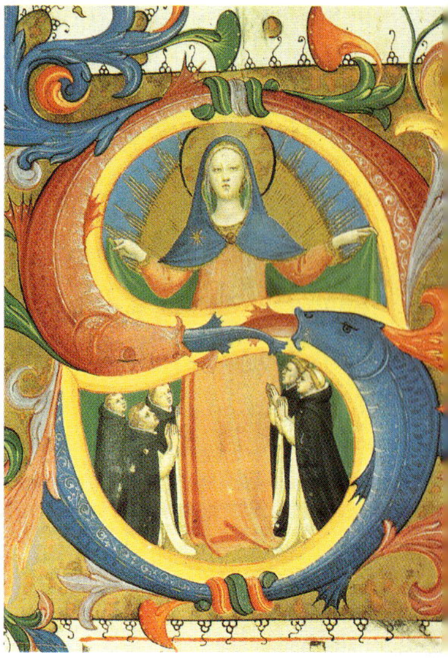

Who were the Observant Dominicans? What role did they play in the religious milieu of Florence in the early 15th century? Already starting from the last years of the 14th century, the so-called "Observances" had been forming within the various monastic orders; these were reformed branches advocating a return to strict respect for the original monastic rules. Their attitude derived from an implicit criticism of that gradual process of secularizing in which, over the years, the various religious groups had moved away from the principles and objectives that had animated their founders. The monastery of San Domenico at Fiesole belonged to the Dominican Observance, a reformed branch of the order established by St Dominic, and was composed of members of the regular clergy. Since they were monks, the brothers were obliged to live in a community, but as Dominicans they had to carry out the ministry of preaching, for which intense study of the Scriptures was required.

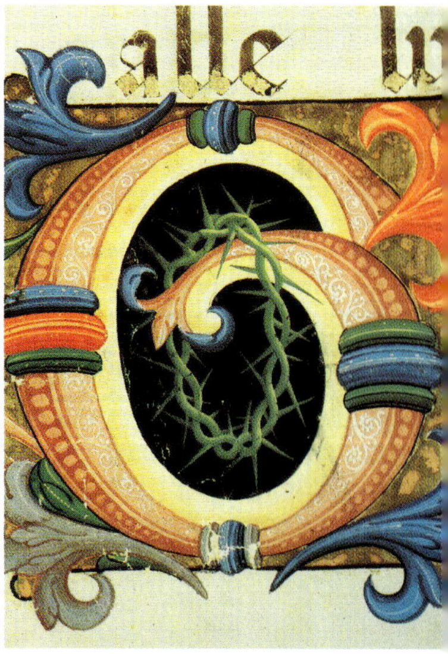

It was therefore an order of highly cultivated preachers, and was perhaps just for this reason more inclined to accept and appreciate one who, among its ranks, by mastering the art of painting, could satisfy in personal but effective manner the need to divulge doctrinarian concepts.

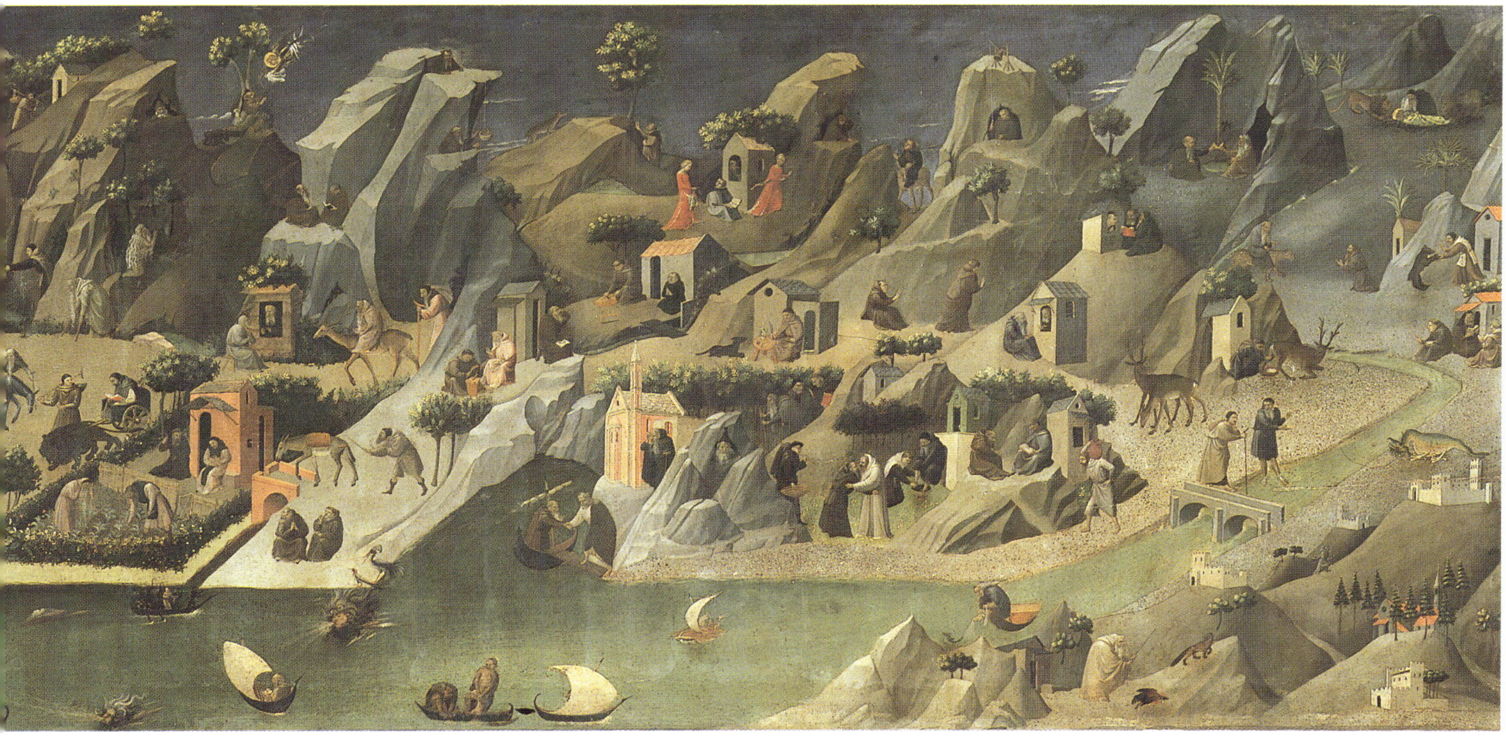

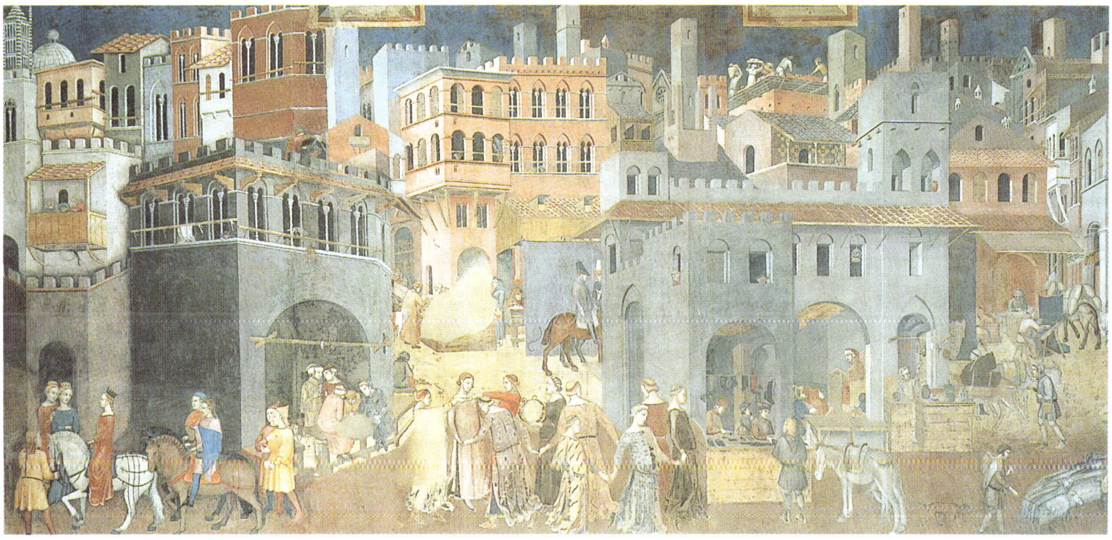

Above:
Thebaide (*Scenes from the life of the hermits living around Thebes*), c. 1420. Florence, Uffizi Gallery.

At right:
The Effects of Good Government, detail from the fresco painted by Ambrogio Lorenzetti in Palazzo Pubblico at Siena, 1338-1340.

The Virgin Patron of the Dominicans and *The Crown of Thorns*, initials decorated by Fra Angelico and Zanobi Strozzi in the *Missal 558*, c. 1425. Florence, San Marco Museum, Library.

The monastery at Fiesole had been rebuilt and enlarged thanks to a favorable environment for the Observances created by Pope Martin V, which was to continue beyond his papacy under his successors Eugene IV and Nicholas V. Very soon Fra Angelico set up a flourishing school of illuminators in the monastery, active in producing not only codices and standards but also more demanding works such as polyptychs and altarpieces. Attributed to this period is the *Missal 558* now in the library of the San Marco Monastery, probably created by Fra Angelico in collaboration with one of his followers, the illuminator Zanobi Strozzi. The chief objective of the monastery workshop must have been that of producing works of both aesthetic and didactic scope, effective liturgical tools serving the theological needs of the order, and not of it alone. We know that Fra Angelico painted for similar purposes works for clients outside his monastery, such as the Canons of Santa Maria del Fiore and the Dominicans of Santa Maria Novella; and that he was further encouraged and supported in this by the general of his own order, Leonardo Dati. It is possible that his superiors themselves collected the proceeds from his works. As a friar, in fact, he would certainly have taken a vow of poverty.

As concerns his early training, it has often been suggested that Fra Angelico may have learned the art of illuminating and panel painting from the Camaldolensian monk Pietro di Giovanni, known as Lorenzo Monaco, a fine miniaturist and late Gothic painter who had been the director of the monastery of Santa Maria degli Angeli, near which Fra Angelico had lived before taking his vows. This vicinity may have facilitated his study of the monk's works, of his techniques and his secrets. But Fra Angelico's first paintings, although showing the influence of the illuminist style, seem already far removed from the language of his presumed master.

Art historians have seen a more likely kinship with the work of Gherardo Starnina, particularly for the acute sensitivity of this painter to light and color. Stylistic affinities between Fra Angelico's youthful works and Starnina's late production are exemplified in a work such as the *Thebaide* now in the Uffizi, which has been alternatively attributed to the two painters. The panel, dating from around 1420, has been identified with a painting listed in the inventory of Palazzo Medici compiled at the death of Lorenzo the Magnificent, and attributed to Fra Angelico. Episodes of the hermits' life set amid the harsh slopes of a rocky landscape of archaic tone closely recall the Sienese frescoes of Ambrogio Lorenzetti entitled *The Effects of Good Government*, while the characters depicted with the skill of a miniaturist and with narrative gusto show a stylistic similarity to the early works of Fra Angelico. Far from certain is the intriguing hypothesis that the panel, perhaps a "spalliera" for one of the rooms in Palazzo Medici, belonged to the father of Cosimo the Elder, who had co-founded with his friend Carlo Guidi the community of the Beggar Hermits of San Gerolamo at Fiesole. In this case, the *Thebaide* would be the precious document of a first contact between Fra Angelico and the Medici family. However, in the lack of definitive proof, its provenance from a Vallombrosian monastic community has been suggested.

Critics have noted how *The Cedri Madonna*, now at Pisa in the National Museum of San Matteo, shows traces, in the delicate features of the face and in the ethereal body of the Virgin, of the possible influence of Masolino on the young Angelico. A pupil of Gherardo Starnina, Masolino had collaborated with Masaccio in the Brancacci Chapel in the Carmine and was thus certainly known and appreciated by Fra Angelico.

The Cedri Madonna, c. 1420. Pisa, San Matteo National Museum.

Art historians consider this work especially important for an understanding of Fra Angelico's early activity. It is still closely linked to the international Gothic style in the predominance of linear graphic elements in the drapery of the Virgin's gown and in its decorative elegance. The gold leaf background of the panel, characteristic of the most ancient devotional tradition, links the *Cedri Madonna* to 14th century works, conferring on it a precious, mystic luminosity.

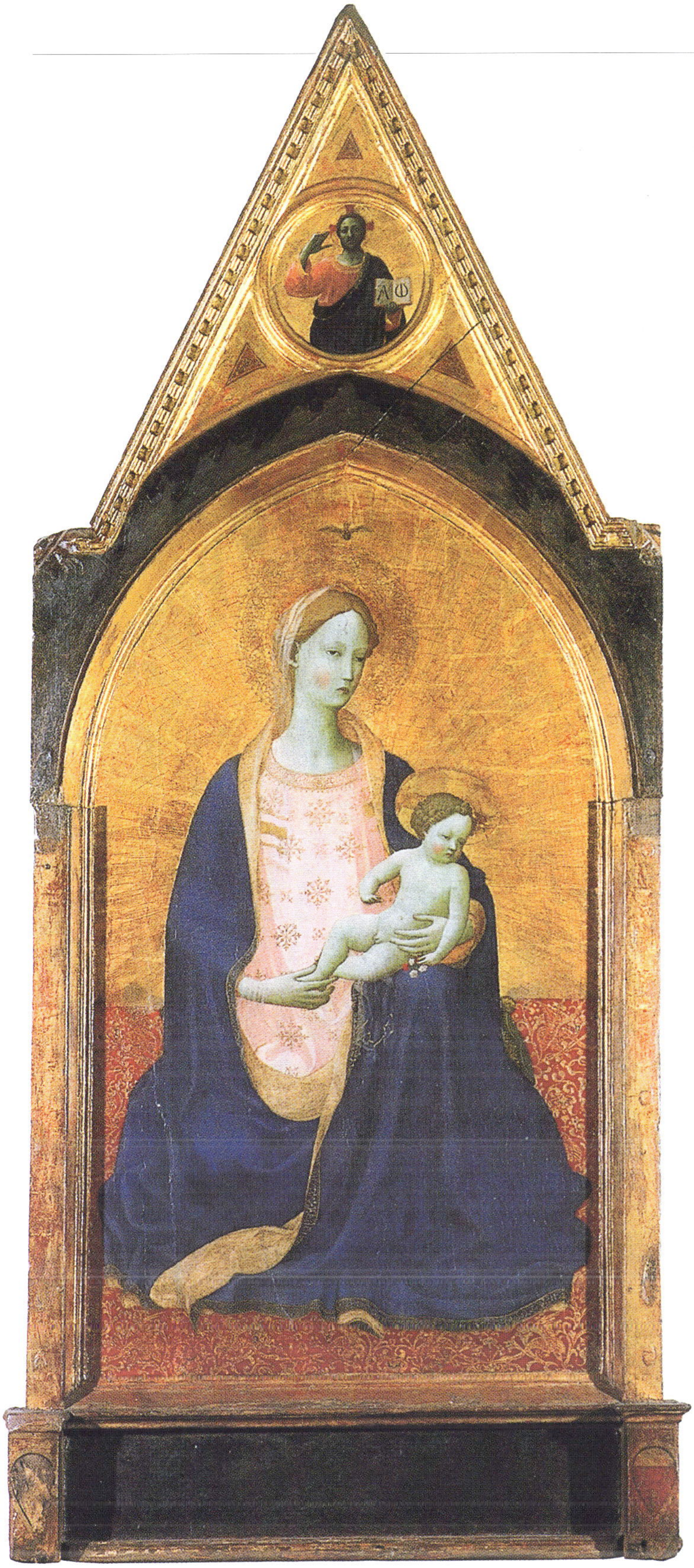

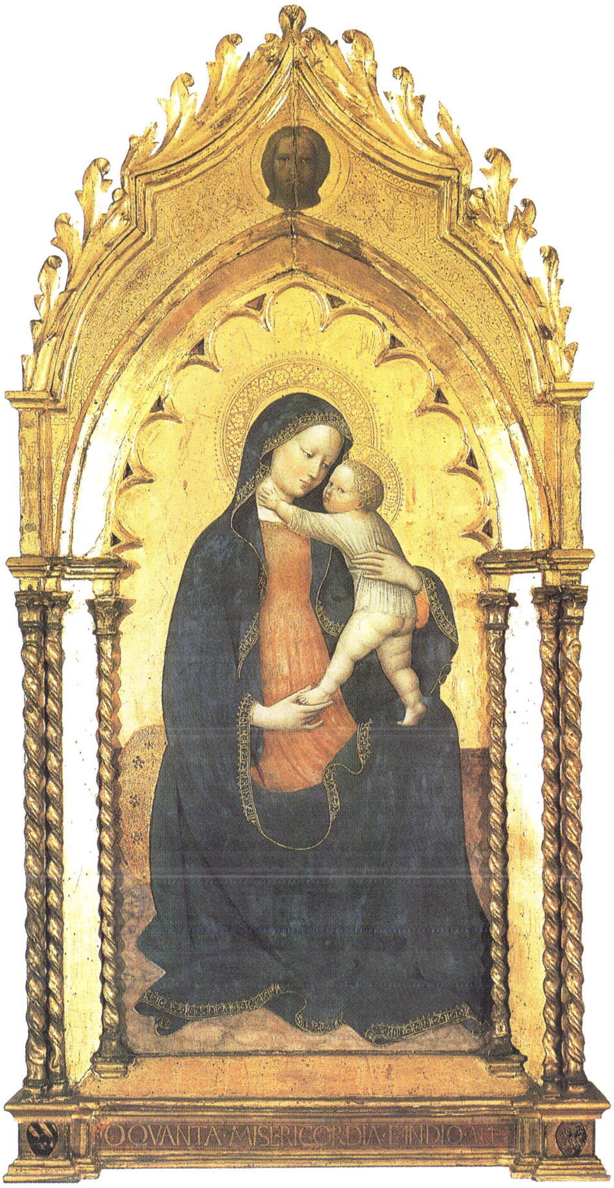

Our Lady of Humility by Masolino, now in the Kunsthalle at Bremen, c. 1423.

But among all of the influences he was surrounded by, the one that most strongly conditioned his pictorial expression was undoubtedly that of Masaccio. From Masaccio, Fra Angelico learned the art of perspective realism, capable of conferring on his mystic, didactic language a new rational force, a communicative power that, by transforming holy events into topical reality, could speak to ecclesiastics and to the faithful in a way not unlike the orations of the Dominican preachers.

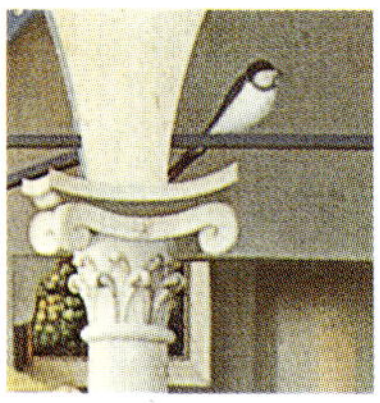

The early works

Dating from the early 1420s, the *San Domenico Altarpiece* painted for the high altar of the church of San Domenico at Fiesole is a key work of Fra Angelico's youth, his first important commission after having taken religious orders. Interpretation of the work today has been rendered difficult by the modifications made in the late 15th century by Lorenzo di Credi, who squared off the painting, eliminating the triptych structure and adding a panel at the top, and then modernized it by painting a landscape over the original gold-leaf background. The figures of the Virgin and the eight angels appear slender and archaic in style, while the more substantial volumes of the saints standing beside the throne seem to reveal Fra Angelico's assimilation of the lesson taught by Masaccio, and the diminishing size of the ornamental polychrome tiles represents a timid attempt at perspective illusion. The seated Virgin is portrayed in the act of offering the Christ Child two roses, one white and one red, symbols of purity and of the Passion, which allude to the Eucharistic theme linked to the collocation of the work over the high altar. In this altarpiece the Virgin is flanked by the figures of St Thomas Aquinas and St Barnabas, St Dominic and St Peter the Martyr. Saints Thomas Aquinas, Dominic and Peter the Martyr are the protectors and founders of the order, while the figure of St Barnabas probably alludes to Barnaba degli Agli, who had left provisions in his will for the work of enlarging and renovating the Fiesole monastery, concluded in 1425. The will, which allocated six thousand florins to the renovating of the Dominican monastery, had been compiled by Leonardo Dati, general of the order, sensitive to the arts and an enlightened patron of Fra Angelico.

Another of Leonardo Dati's initiatives was that of founding the convent of San Pietro Martire, the first Observance convent of the women's order, for which Fra Angelico painted the *San Pietro Martire Triptych*, now in the San Marco Museum. This is probably the painting referred to in a

San Domenico Altarpiece (*Madonna and Child with Eight Angels and Sts Thomas, Barnabas, Dominic and Peter the Martyr*), 1420-1424. Fiesole, San Domenico.

This work represents a milestone in Fra Angelico's youthful production. It clearly shows his innovational spirit, especially considering that it was painted during the same years as the *Adoration of the Magi* by Gentile da Fabriano. The life-like volumes of the saints are a significant indication of the painter's attention to the work of Masaccio. Art historians have noted an affinity between this altarpiece and the *San Giovenale Triptych* painted by Masaccio now in the church of San Pietro a Cascia.

document from 1429 which certifies the existence of a debt owed by the nuns of St Peter the Martyr to the monastery in Fiesole, Fra Angelico's monastery. The work, dating from around the middle of the 1420s, portrays at center the Madonna and Child in majesty. Recognizable beside her are St Dominic, St John the Baptist, St Peter the Martyr and St Thomas. In its structure divided into pinnacled compartments the polyptych still reflects the late Gothic style, echoed also in the gilding and the ornate fabrics, while the scaled positioning of the saints and their plasticity reveal the artist's careful study of scientific perspective. The strong, firm volumetric effect of the Virgin seated on her throne recalls Masaccio's *St Anne Metterza*, which hung at the time in the church of Sant'Ambrogio and is

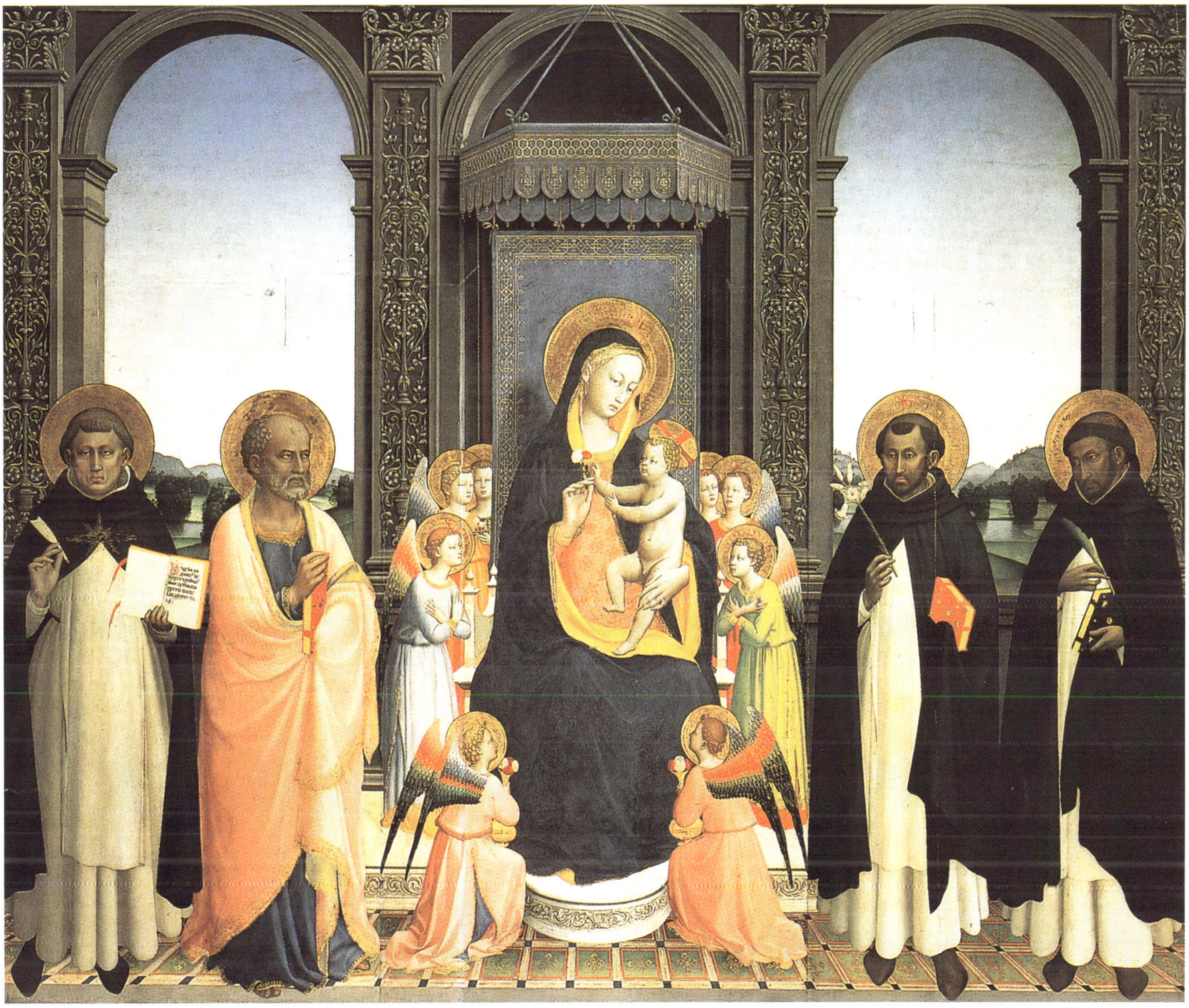

now in the Uffizi Gallery. Late Gothic echoes seem to re-emerge in the figures appearing in the medallions in the pinnacles – the angel, the Eternal and Our Lady of the Annunciation – and in the panel applied above them which, in the language of the miniaturist, narrates stories of St Peter the

Martyr. Viewed from nearby they recall the work of Gentile da Fabriano, who was active in Florence at the time in the churches of Santa Trinita and San Niccolò Sopr'Arno.

Also dating from the middle of the 1420s is the *Annunciation* of Madrid, which came in the distant past from the church of San Domenico at Fiesole. The painting is probably one of the two altarpieces executed for the Gaddi family, wealthy merchants who were descendents of the 14th century painter Taddeo Gaddi and the owners of two side chapels in the Fiesole church. The original collocation of the altarpiece is a confirmation of the painter's good reputation not only in ecclesiastical spheres but also among the wealthy Florentine upper class, which frequently commissioned works of religious subject. In the composition, the Virgin's chamber opens onto a portico held up by slender columns, an elegant architectural link between the interior of the house and the exterior where a flourishing garden reminiscent of Eden, abounding in flowers and plants, is described with an analytic spirit that recalls the late Gothic style of Gentile da Fabriano. Here the grieving figures of Adam and Eve driven out of the earthly paradise represent Original sin, while the Announcement of the coming of Christ heralds his mission of redeeming mankind. The portrayal of the expulsion from the earthly paradise in the Madrid altarpiece seems a sort of citation of the progenitors painted a few years earlier by Masaccio on the walls of the Brancacci Chapel. Masaccio's influence tinged with accents from Gentile da Fab-

San Pietro Martire Triptych (Madonna and Child with Sts Dominic, John the Baptist, Peter the Martyr and Thomas Aquinas), whole and details of the cusps with *The preaching and the death of St Peter the Martyr*, 1424-1425. Florence, San Marco Museum.

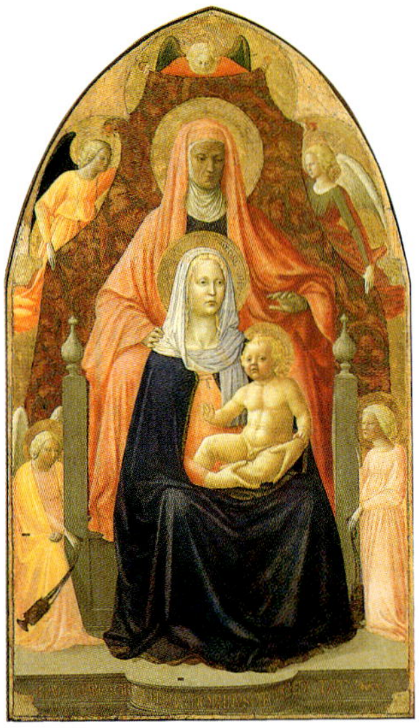

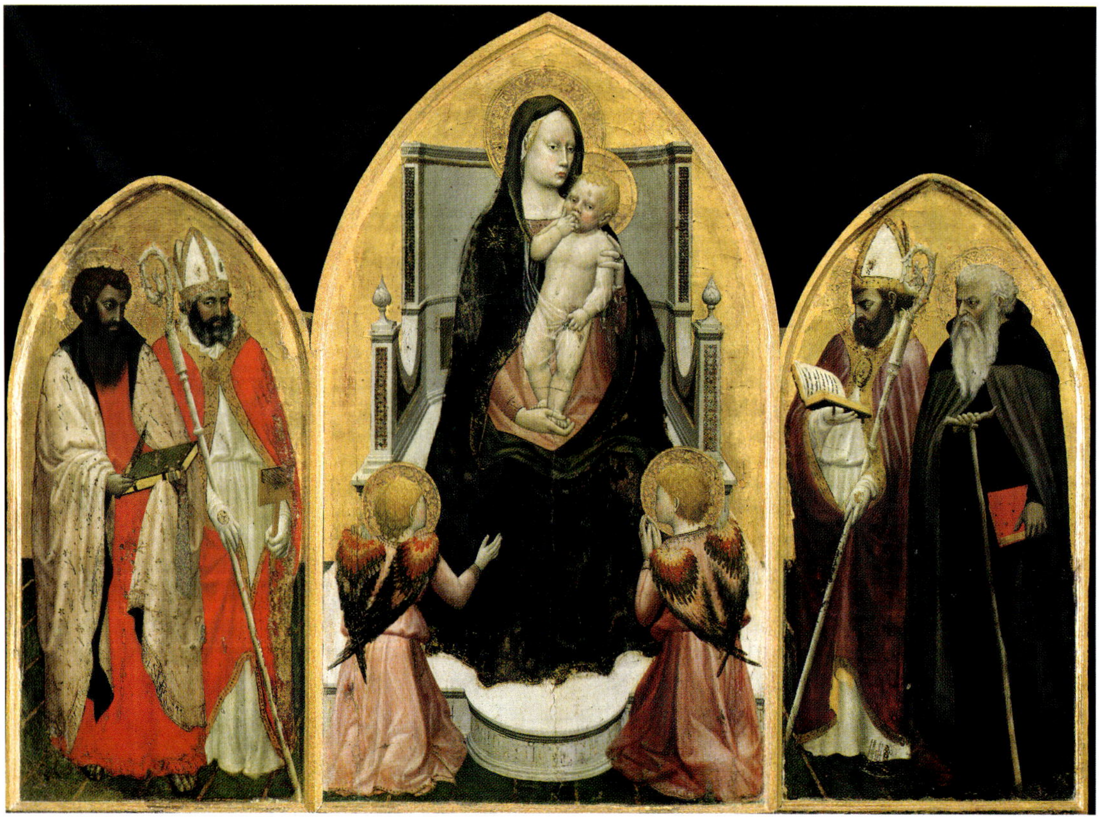

Above:
St Anne Metterza by Masolino and Masaccio, now in the Uffizi Gallery, 1424-1425.

At left:
San Giovenale Triptych by Masaccio, in the Pieve di San Pietro at Cascia di Reggello (Province of Florence), 1422.

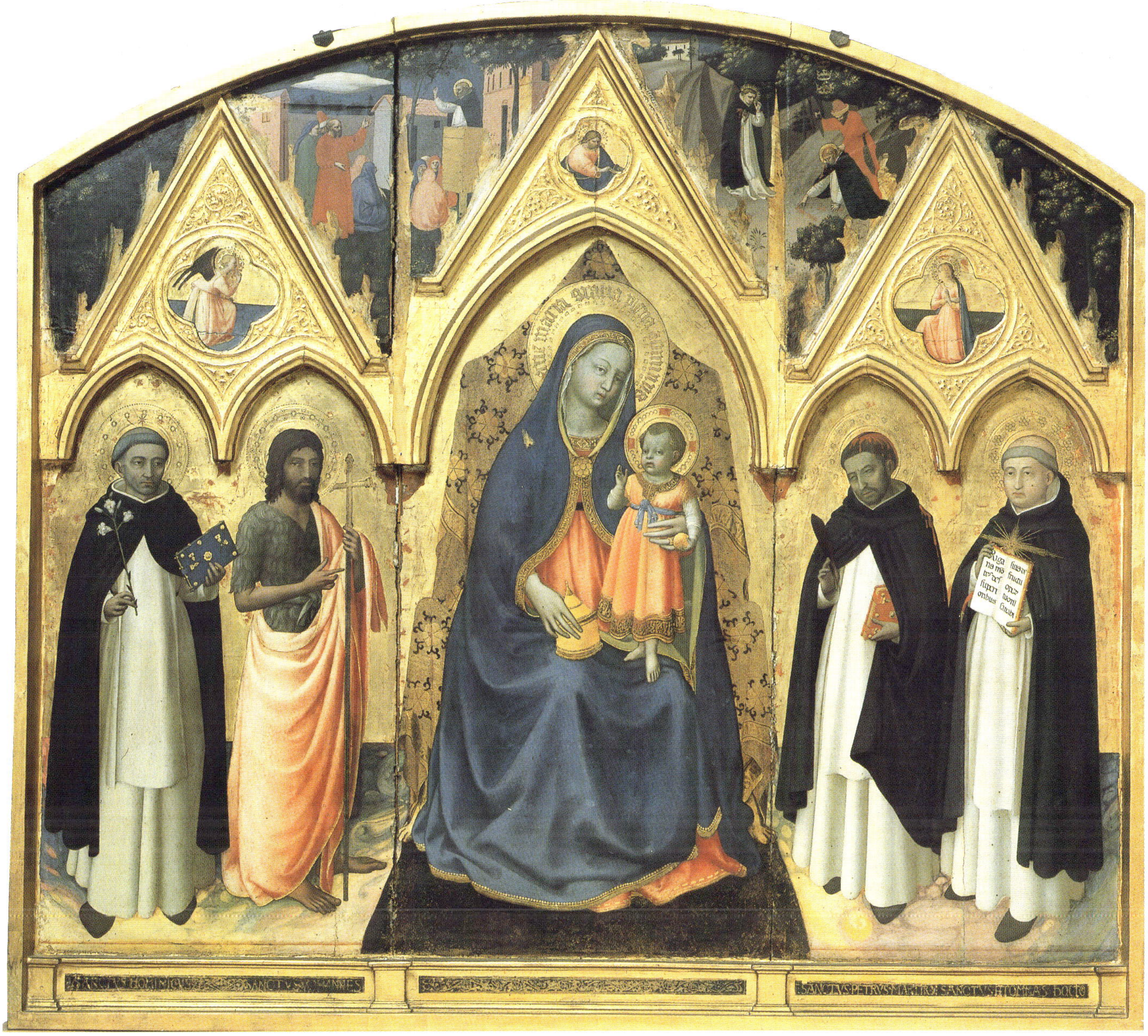

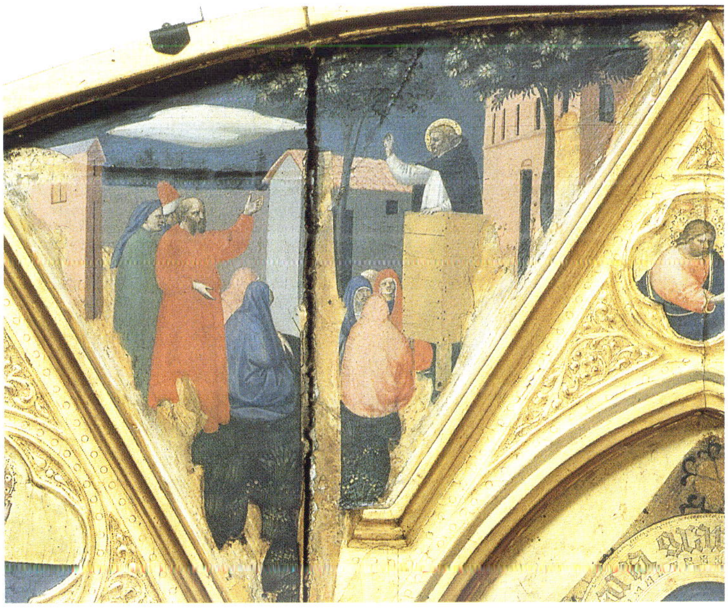

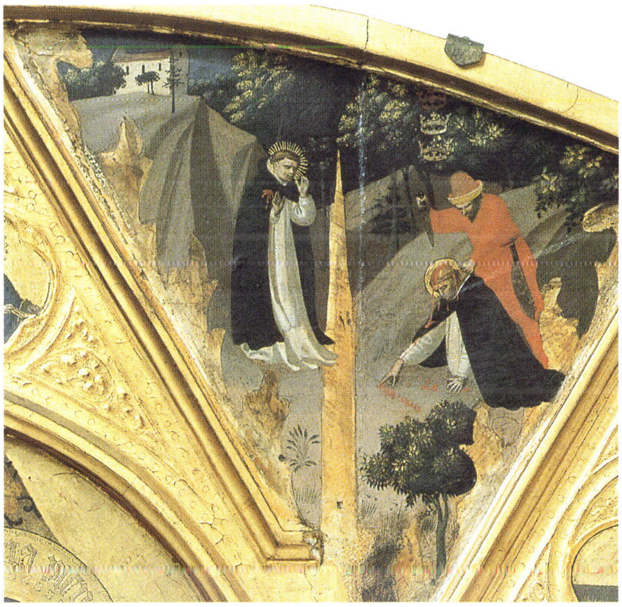

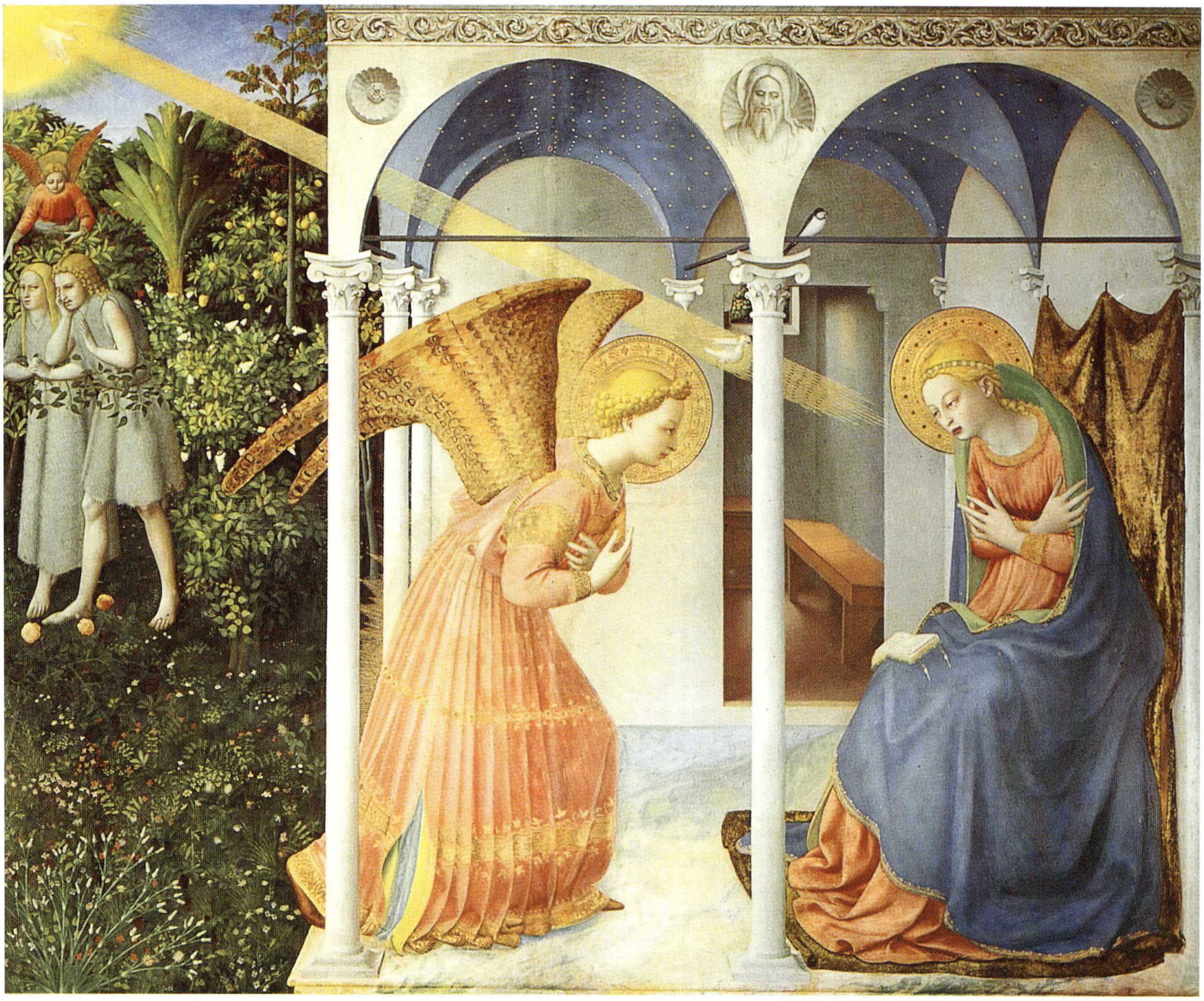

riano appears to distinguish a series of works attributable to the second half of the 1420s and very probably painted for the Dominican Giovanni Masi. These are four small tabernacle-reliquaries, painted and destined to hold sacred relics within the same frame. Masi was the sacristan of the Dominican church of Santa Maria Novella. The *Chronicles* of the church relate in fact that he placed in the sacristy four small panels painted by Fra Giovanni da Fiesole and adorned "with beautiful figures of Mary Virgin and of the Angel Saints". Among these was the precious *Madonna of the Star*, now in the San Marco Museum. Here an architectural aedicule crowned by spires and decorated with late Gothic rosettes presents at its center a statuary Madonna and Child, whose three-dimensional effect is enhanced by the beautifully painted chiaroscuro of the folds in her mantle.

Also dating from the second half of the 1420s is the *Last Judgement* in the San Marco Museum, one of Fra Angelico's most famous paintings. This work had been painted by the artist for the church of Santa Maria degli Angeli, the residence of the Camaldolensian monk Ambrogio Traversari, friend

Annunciation, 1425-1426. Madrid, Prado.

The many species of plants illustrated with analytic care in late Gothic style refer to the episode in which the Archangel announces the coming of Christ. A ray of mystic golden light coming from the hand of the Eternal thrusts the Holy Ghost toward the praying Mary and represents, with a symbol dear to the Holy Scriptures, divine intervention.

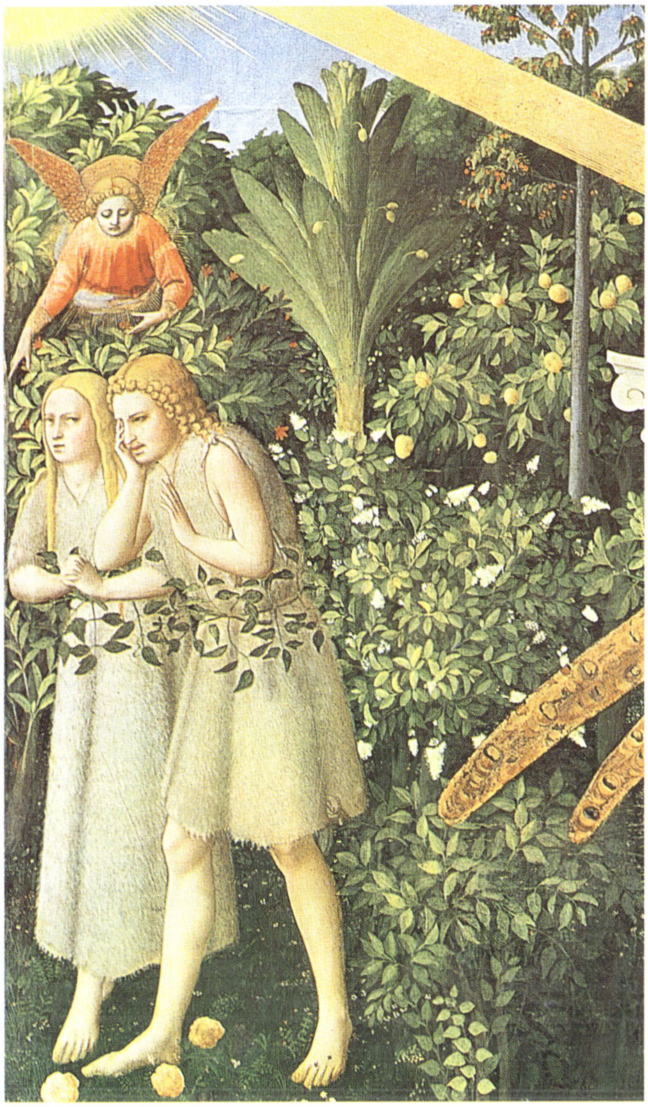

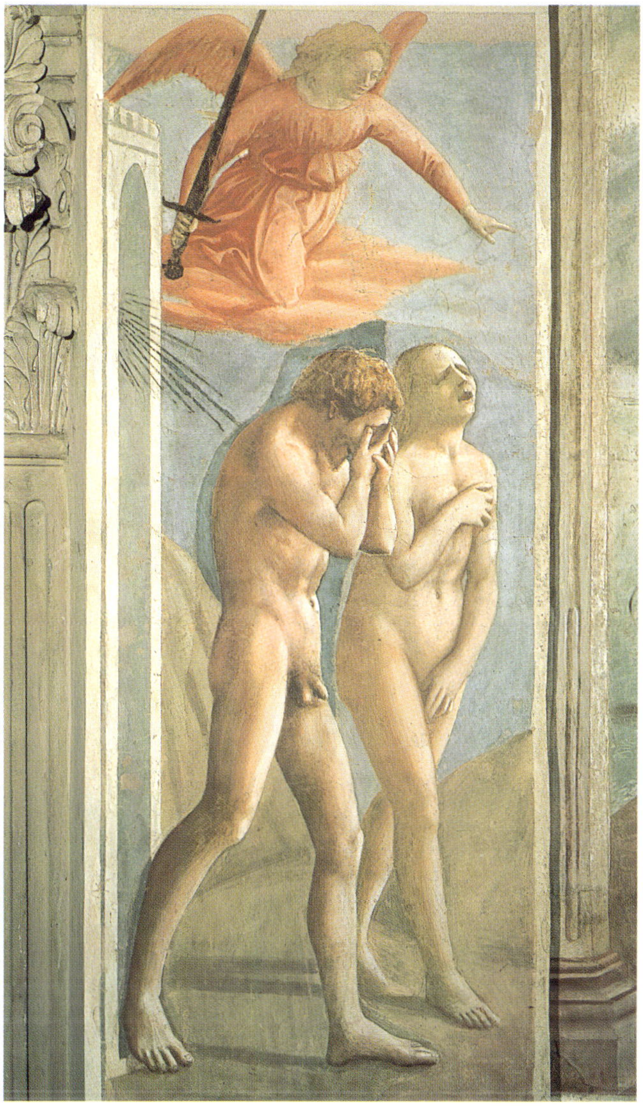

Annunciation, detail of *Adam and Eve*, 1425-1426. Madrid, Prado.

The Expulsion of Adam and Eve frescoed by Masaccio in the Brancacci Chapel cycle in Santa Maria del Carmine, Florence, 1424-1425.

of the humanist Niccolò Niccoli and founder in his own monastery of an academy of Greek and Latin studies. The theologian was deeply learned in Greek patristics and it may have been at his suggestion that Fra Angelico inserted in the complex iconography of the painting the figures of Abraham, David and Aaron, with other personages from the Old Testament, in the place customarily reserved to the Apostles in traditional Christian iconography, that is, standing beside Christ the Judge. Among those unusual presences are many saints of the Eastern Church, apparently grouped at random, along with saints from the Western Church. Subtly but clearly there emerges from these iconographic choices the ecumenical ideal of which Traversari was in those years one of the chief promoters. The pictorial language of the work is marked by both archaic and innovative features. While, in fact, 14th century citations are not lacking, such as glimpses of flowery nature, the damned tortured by demons and a unitary spatial concept, emphasized by the line of open tombs in perspective, the style derives once more from a personal meditation on Masaccio's discoveries. And while

Madonna of the Star (Madonna and Child, the Eternal, Angels and Dominican Saints), c. 1427. Florence, San Marco Museum.

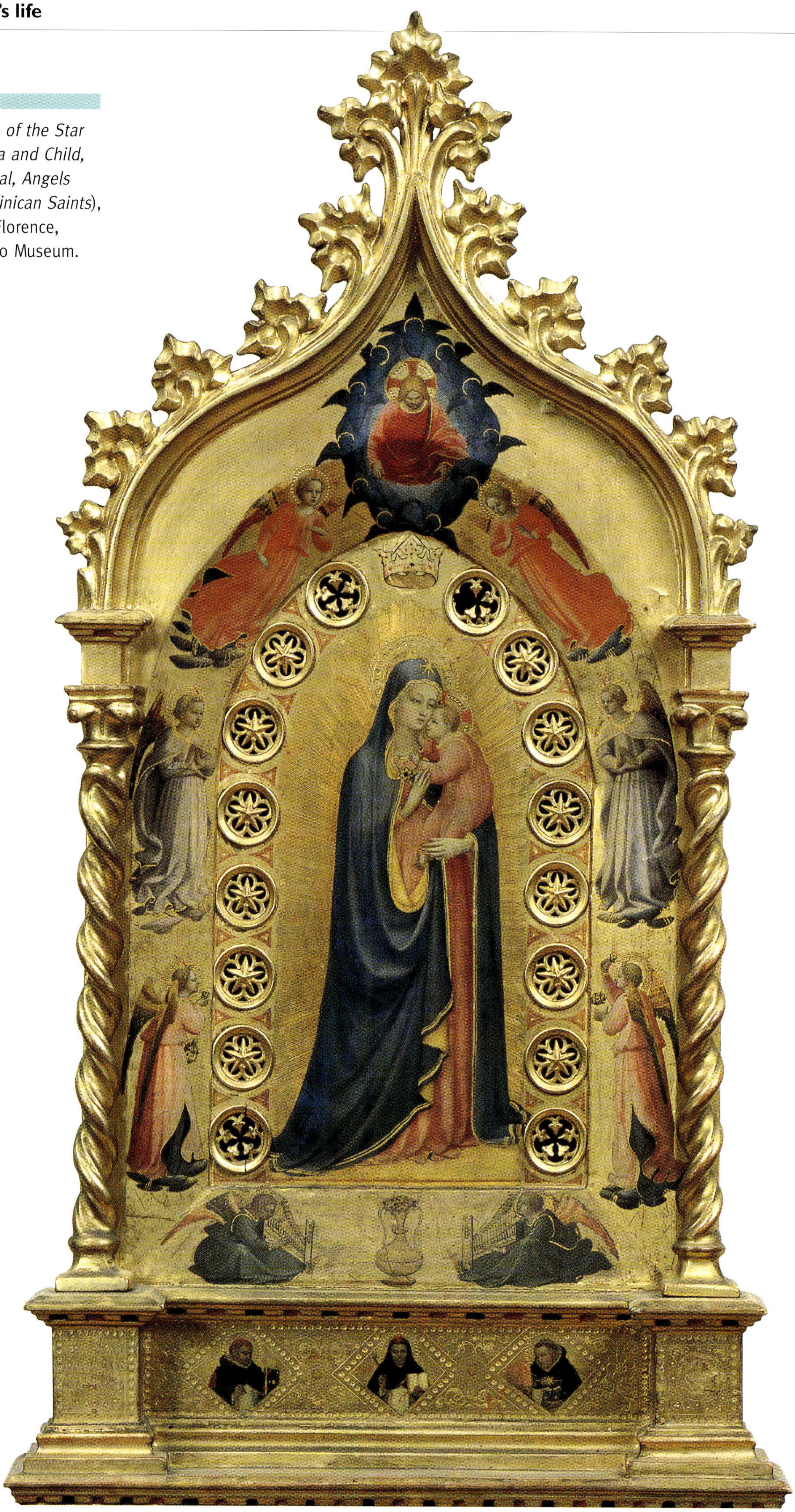

Coronation of the Virgin, Adoration of the Christ Child and Angels, c. 1430. Florence, San Marco Museum.

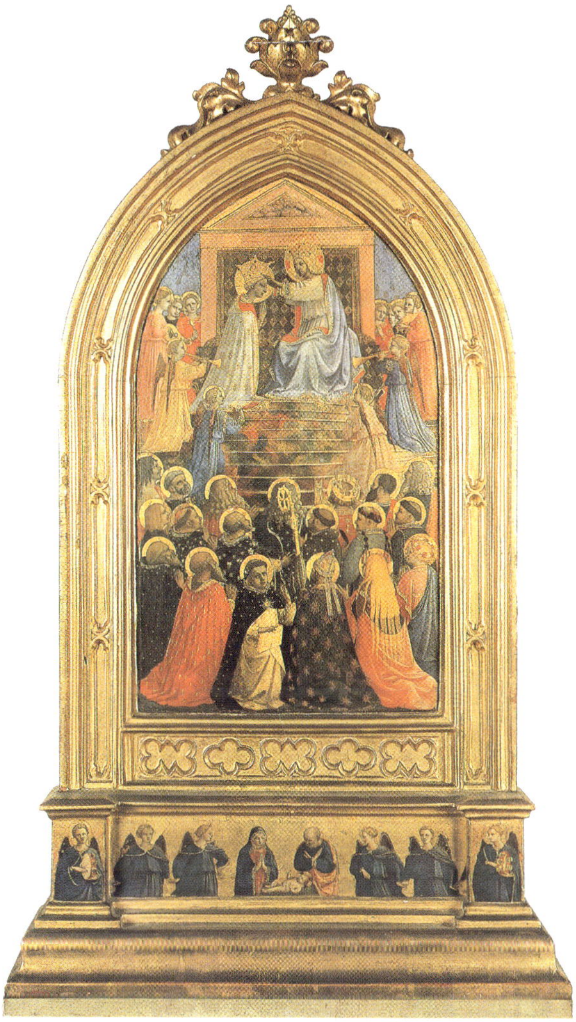

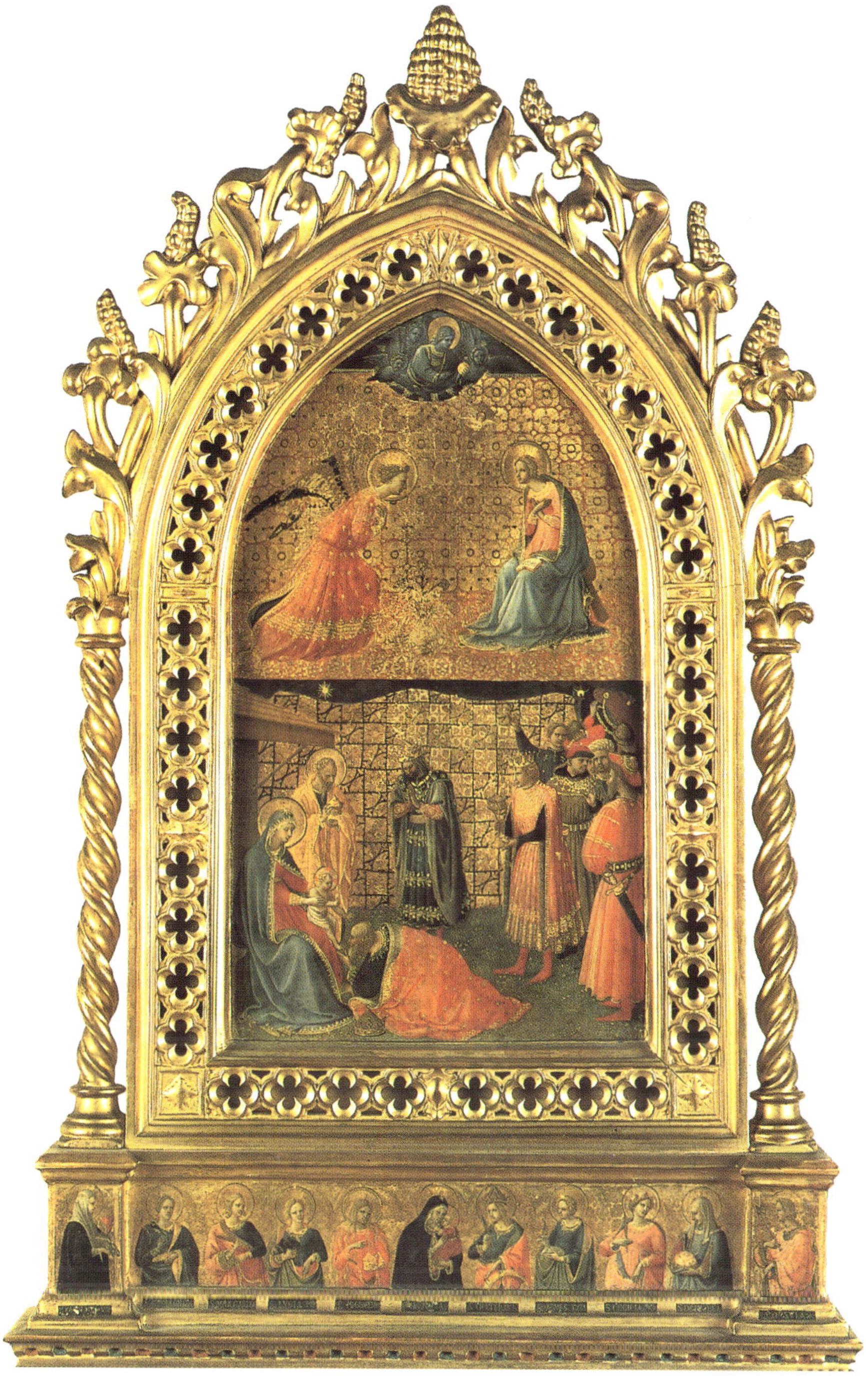

Upper right: *Annunciation, Adoration of the Magi, Madonna and Saints,* c. 1428. Florence, San Marco Museum.

the figure of Christ in a mandorla of gilded rays closely recalls coeval miniatures, the gesture of the Pantocrator's hands, one turned upward, the other downward to express the salvation or condemnation of those judged, is a magnificently innovative iconographic expedient. Intensely symbolic is the abundant use of rays of gilded light, mystic metaphors for the divine light.

Coming, like the Madrid *Annunciation*, from a partition in the church of San Domenico at Fiesole, the *Coronation of the Virgin* now in the Louvre (see pp. 48-49) represents one of the masterpieces of Fra Angelico dating from around the beginning of the century's third decade. In it, perspective virtuosity is accompanied by extreme care taken in minute attention to each decorative detail. A warm, mystic light envelops the entire scene, making its colors glow like precious stones.

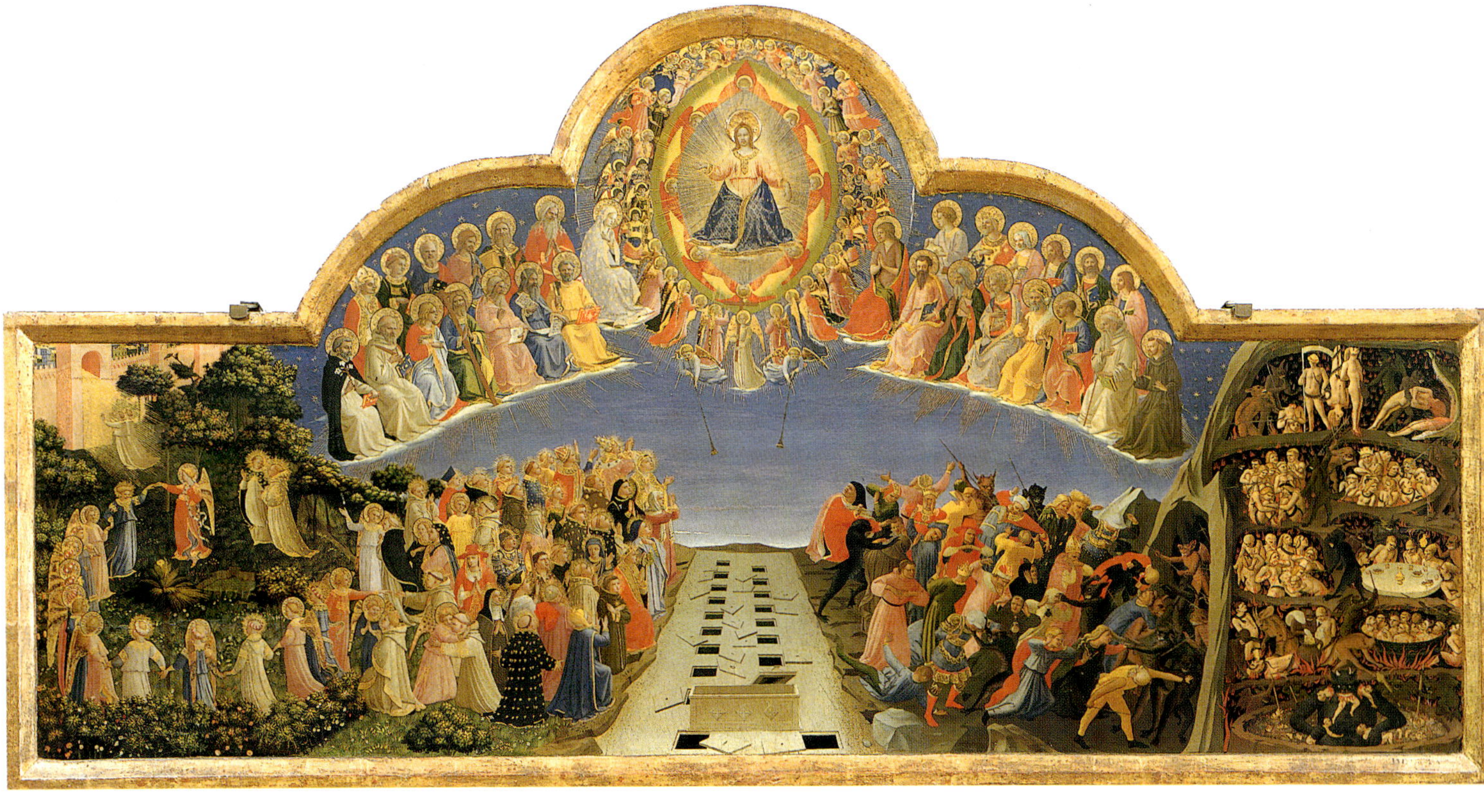

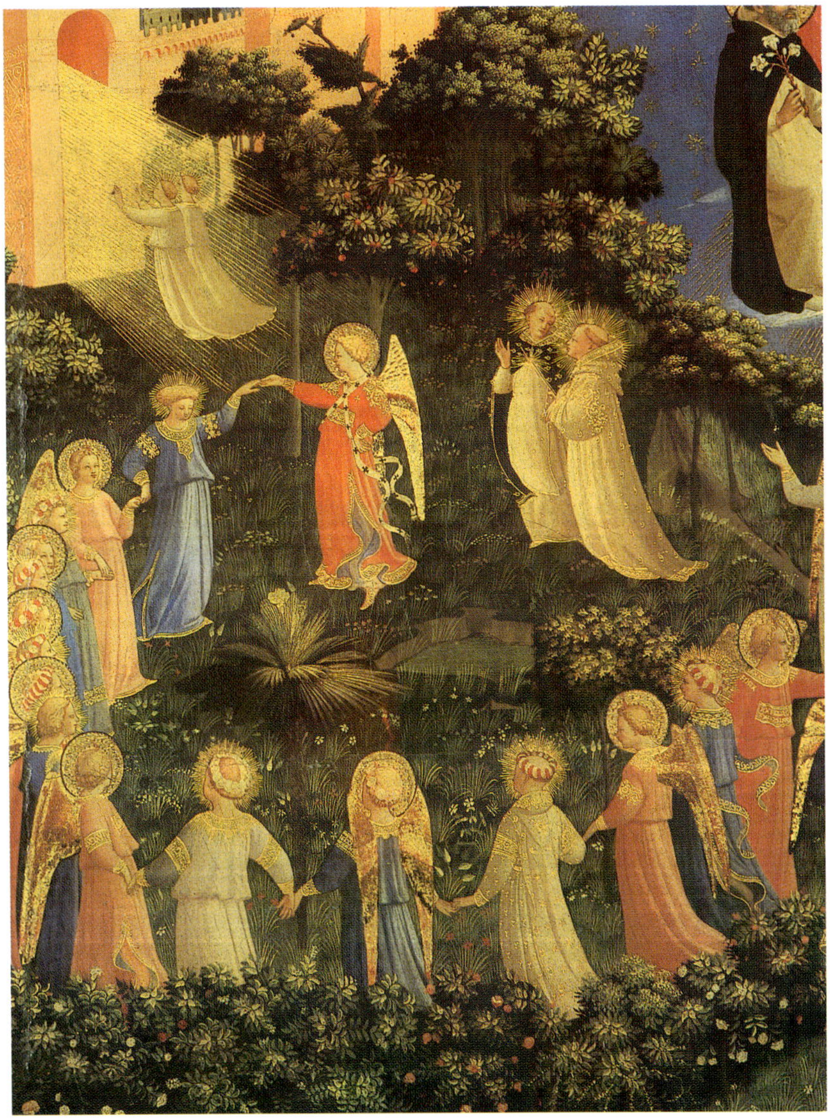

The Last Judgement, whole and details, 1425-1430. Florence, San Marco Museum.

The painting presents a large number of personages and iconographical details dense in significance, showing that it was painted for a highly cultivated patron, the Humanist monk Ambrogio Traversari, Prior of the Camaldolensian monastery of Santa Maria degli Angeli. The crude tones used to describe hell and the damned vividly contrast in archaic style with the elegiac accents of paradise. Here the angels dance in a graceful circle against the background of luxurious vegetation illustrated in late Gothic style. Those judged worthy of salvation are depicted in various attitudes and characterized by gowns and headgear of widely varying styles and colors, while on the opposite side of the painting the condemned, with horrified faces and expressive gestures, are thrust by demons toward the inside of an infernal cavern. The touches of gold on both sides of the work seem to become more intense on the gowns of the elect, visually emphasizing their mystic contact with the Eternal.

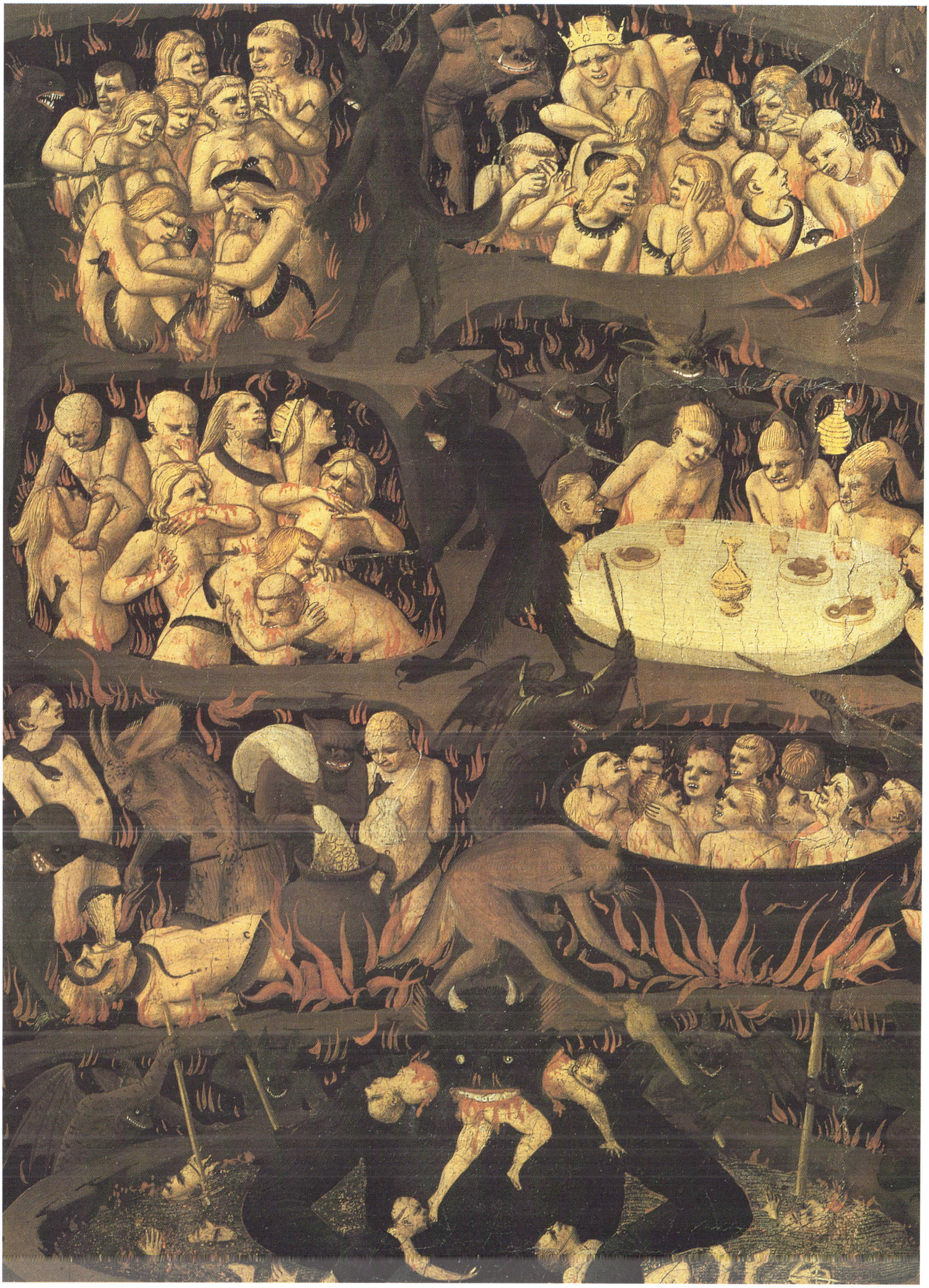

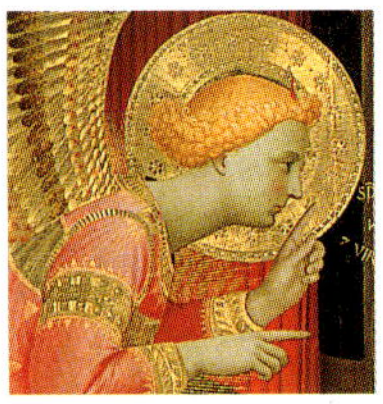

Masterpieces of the artist's maturity

Cristoforo Landino, in the late 15th century, defined Fra Angelico's way of painting as "devout and affected and highly ornate, done with great ease". While the terms "affected" and "ornate" allude to a style which is delicate and attentive to decorative details, "devout" seems to refer not so much to the form as to the content of the paintings: to the subjects and the way in which they are represented. The artist's use of an iconography which is often unexpectedly precious has suggested to art historians the need for further study of Fra Angelico's work in relation to the erudite milieu of the Dominican Observance and the Humanist inclinations of many of the order's leading figures.

It was in early 15th century Florence, in fact, that there was formulated the Humanist ideal of a Church in which the study of pagan Antiquity as the golden age of thought and the study of the Holy Scriptures were not conflicting terms, but instead concurred in recalling the Church to the spirituality of its origins. The Humanist Coluccio Salutati ardently sustained that classical studies were necessary to the intellectual and moral formation of the young and even that these *studia humanitatis* were so closely connected with *studia divinitatis* that true knowledge could not be attained if one of these two elements were missing. A significant part of *studia humanitatis* consisted of the arts of the trivium (grammar, logic and rhetoric), which were based on reading the works of the great poets, historians and philosophers of Greek and Latin antiquity. To them St Augustine had already in the past acknowledged the function of furnishing the tools necessary for an understanding of the Scriptures.

A Humanist and Dominican preacher was Antonino Pierozzi, Prior of the monastery at Fiesole at the time when Fra Angelico entered the monastic community, and later to become Archbishop of Florence. In his erudite preaching emerged the idea that the art of painting was closely linked to the

The Naming of the Baptist, c. 1430. Florence, San Marco Museum.

This painting, always considered one of Fra Angelico's most characteristic works, was originally one of the sections of a predella. It represents the episode in which Zechariah, struck dumb as punishment for his disbelief at the announcement of the conception of John the Baptist, writes on a sheet of paper the name to be given his newborn son. The atmosphere is solemn but the touches of daily realism closely recall the style of Masaccio. The checkered wall shows Fra Angelico's interest in architecture. The scene is bathed in a warm sunny light, mystic and at the same time realistic.

practice of contemplation, according to the principle that the vision of images could lead, by analogy, to a wholly spiritual vision. As rhetoric in the art of oration conferred beauty on words and force on thought, so painting, through the skilful use of color, light and images, was acknowledged the ability to confer form and beauty on religious concepts for the purpose of inducing the faithful to contemplation of a higher order. The concept of painting as noble rhetoric could not fail to meet with the wholehearted acceptance of a Dominican painter, for whom devotion and inspiration were indissoluble elements, crucially important to the charisma of the order itself. Fra Angelico thus became the interpreter of a world of religious images influenced by the thought of the great preachers of the time such as Leonardo Dati, Am-

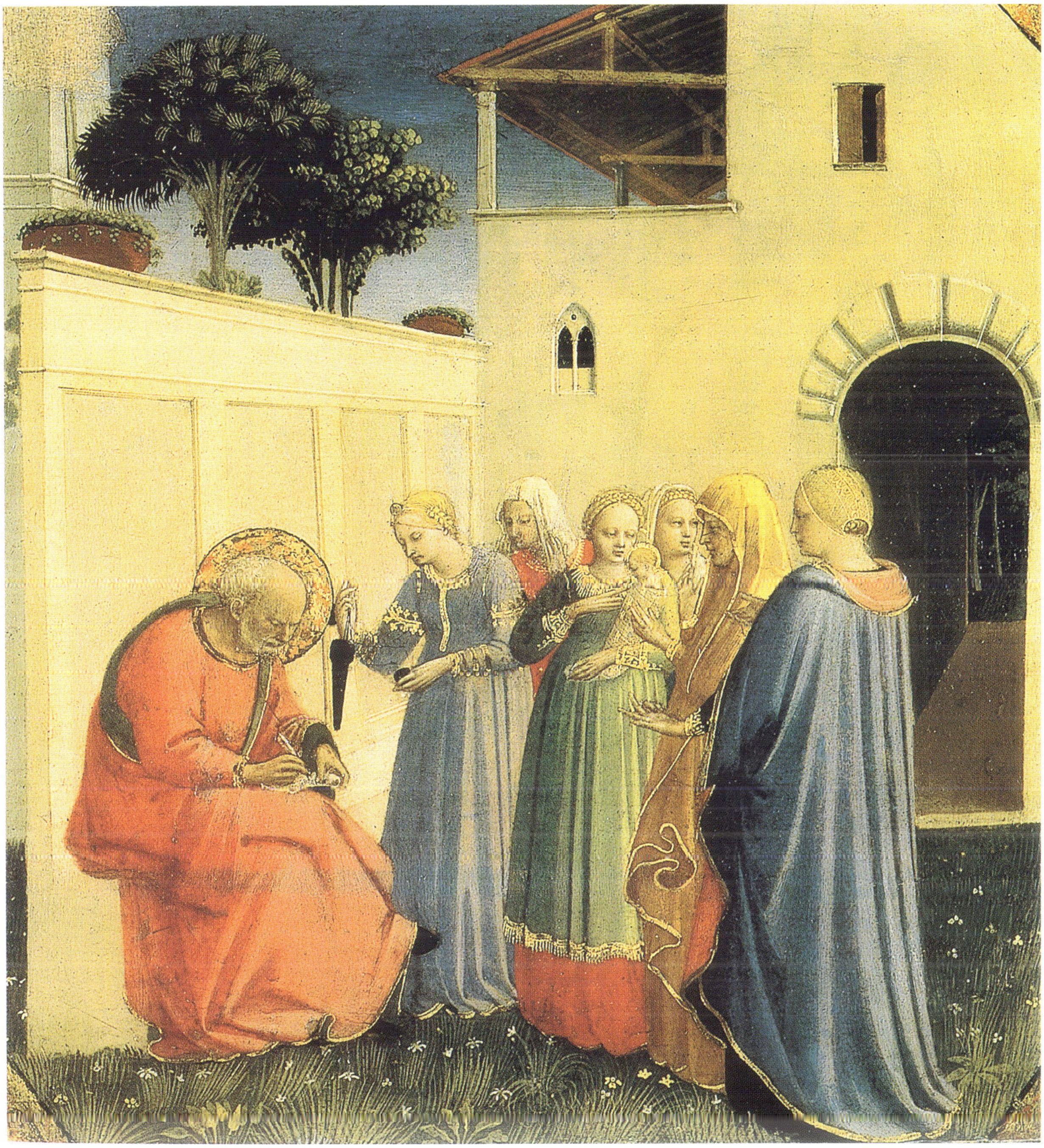

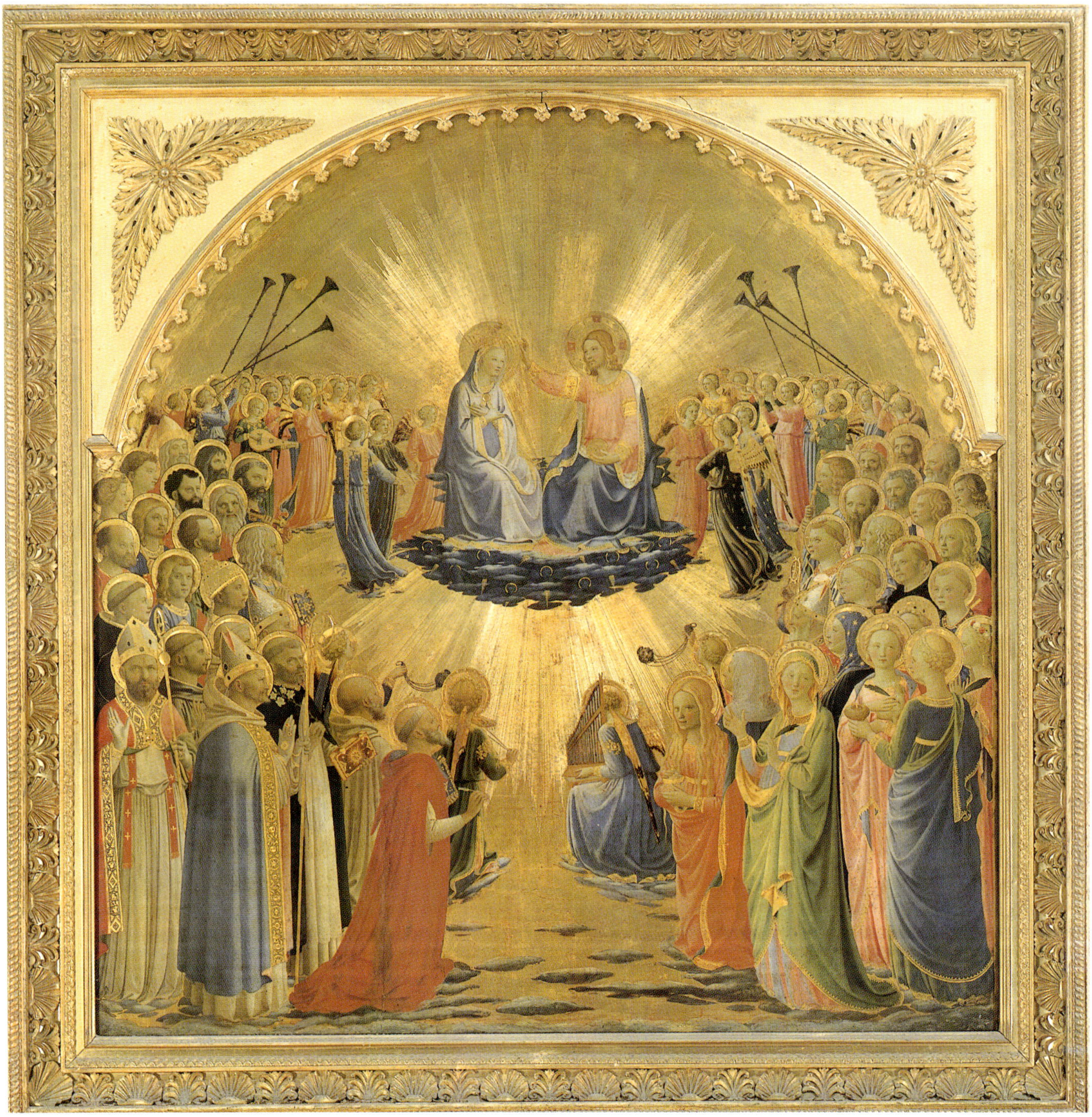

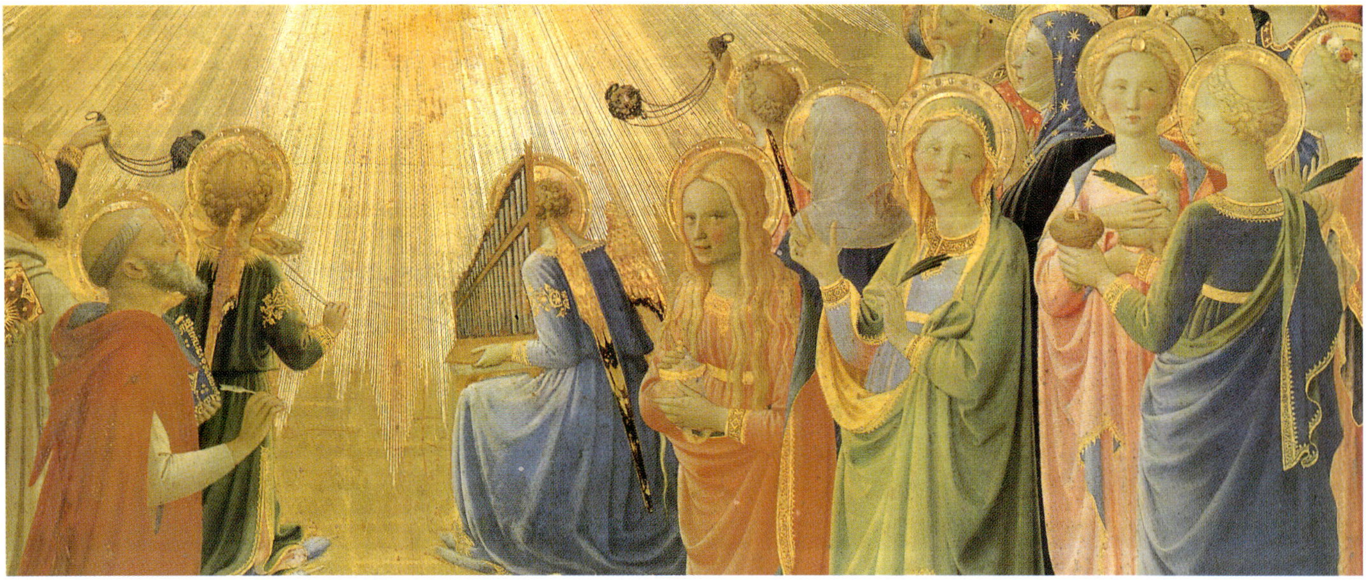

Coronation of the Virgin, whole and detail, c. 1432. Florence, Uffizi Gallery.

brogio Traversari, Antonino Pierozzi and the Humanists such as Niccolò Niccoli and Coluccio Salutati, and the messenger of the new Christian Humanism. An expression of this noble rhetoric is the *Deposition* painted for the sacristy of the church of Santa Trinita, now in the San Marco Museum (see pp. 50-51). The client for this work was a prominent citizen, Palla Strozzi, a

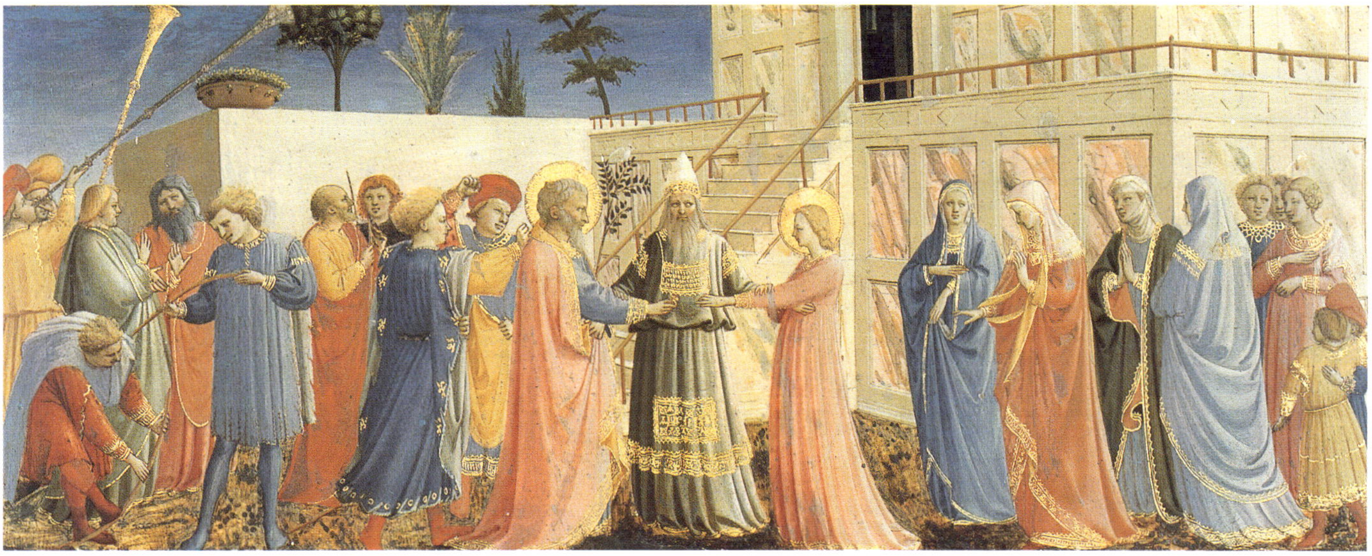

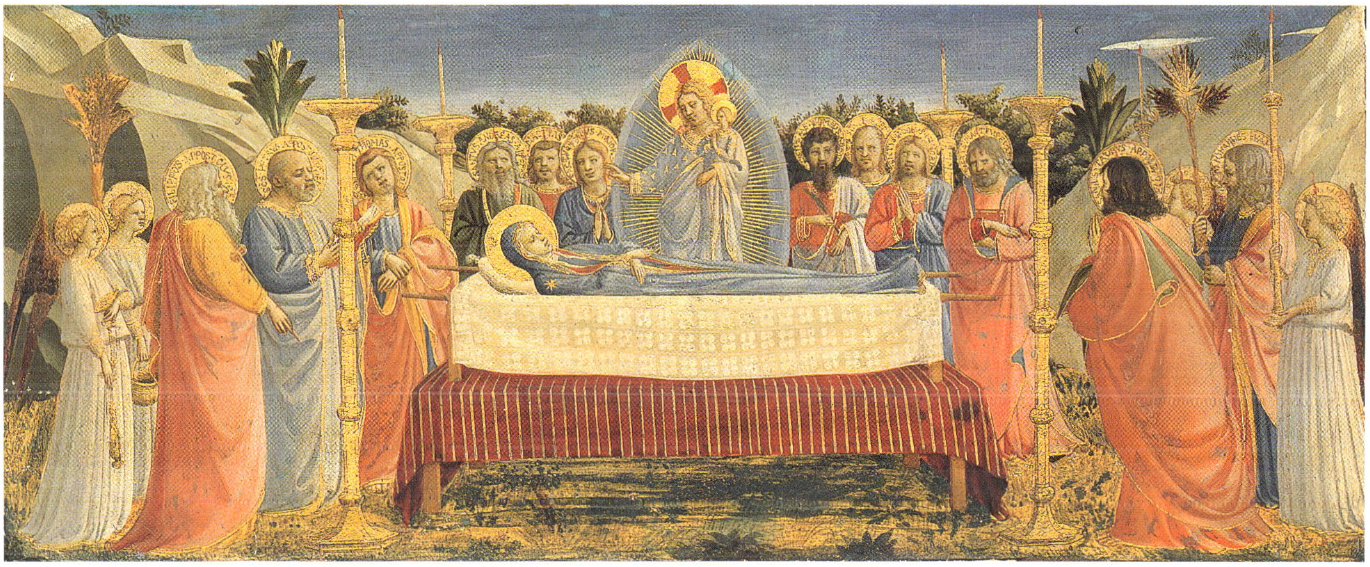

Above: *Marriage of the Virgin* and *Dormitio Virginis*, details from the predella of the *Coronation of the Virgin* now in the Uffizi, c. 1432. Florence, San Marco Museum.

wealthy banker and ardent collector of Greek and Latin codices. Desirous of finding a fitting place for his precious collection, Strozzi had originally intended to donate a library to the church of Santa Trinita but in 1434 he was sentenced to exile and had to leave this ambitious project unfulfilled. The sacristy of Santa Trinita, planned by Palla also as a funeral hall for his father, was divided into two parts, one of which housed the *Adoration of the Magi* by Gentile da Fabriano, now in the Uffizi, the other the *Deposition* by Fra Angelico. Angelico's work, distinguished by the grandiosity of its composition, appears emblematic of his style, "ornate" and at the same time "devout". Statuary figures are placed in a barely suggested triptych structure which, by framing the space, seems to impose on it a rhythm, but without detriment to the overall unity of the composition and the naturalness of the landscape forming the background. The inscriptions in Greek, Latin and Hebrew, precise scriptural references which comment on the entire scene, allude to the client's philological and erudite interests while emphasizing Fra Angelico's theological culture. The onlookers and the main actors in the holy

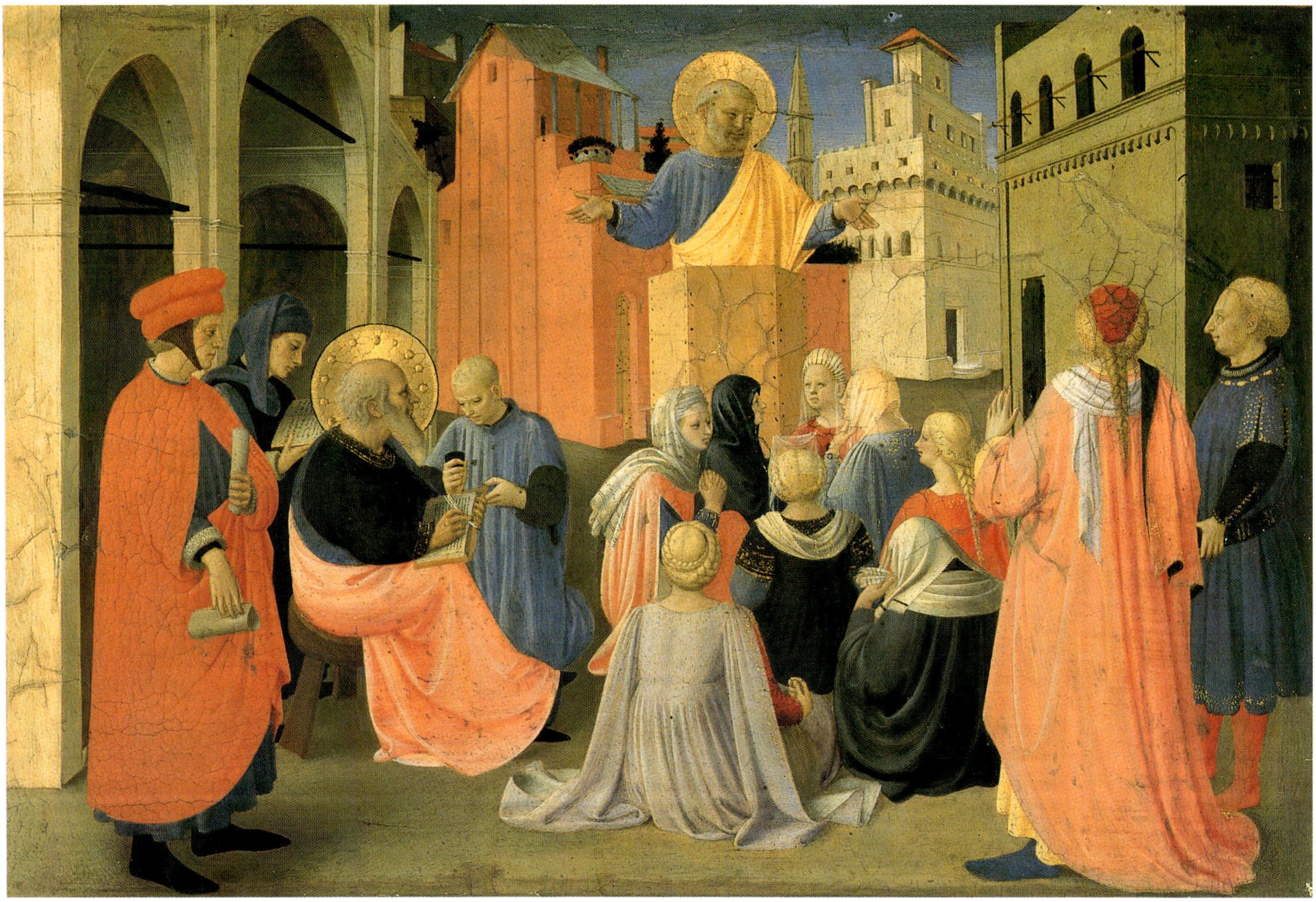

St Peter preaching in the presence of St Mark, detail from the predella of the *Tabernacle of the Linen Drapers*, 1433-1435. Florence, San Marco Museum.

drama are gathered together on a crowded stage. Some of the faces present the distinctive features of portraits. The female personages, positioned at left, have a sculptural aspect and drapery of Ghibertian memory, while the composition of the four figures on the staircase is varied and complex. The monumental style and intensely symbolic gestures confer on the work the characteristics of a moving sermon of high rhetorical value, a worthy translation into painting of Dominican eloquence. Close in style to the *Deposition* and dating from the first years of the fourth decade is the *Coronation of the Virgin* for the choir of the nuns of Sant'Egidio, the church of the hospital of Santa Maria Nuova, and now in the Uffizi.

In 1433, Fra Angelico's leading position among the Florentine artists of the fourth decade was confirmed by a commission from the Arte dei

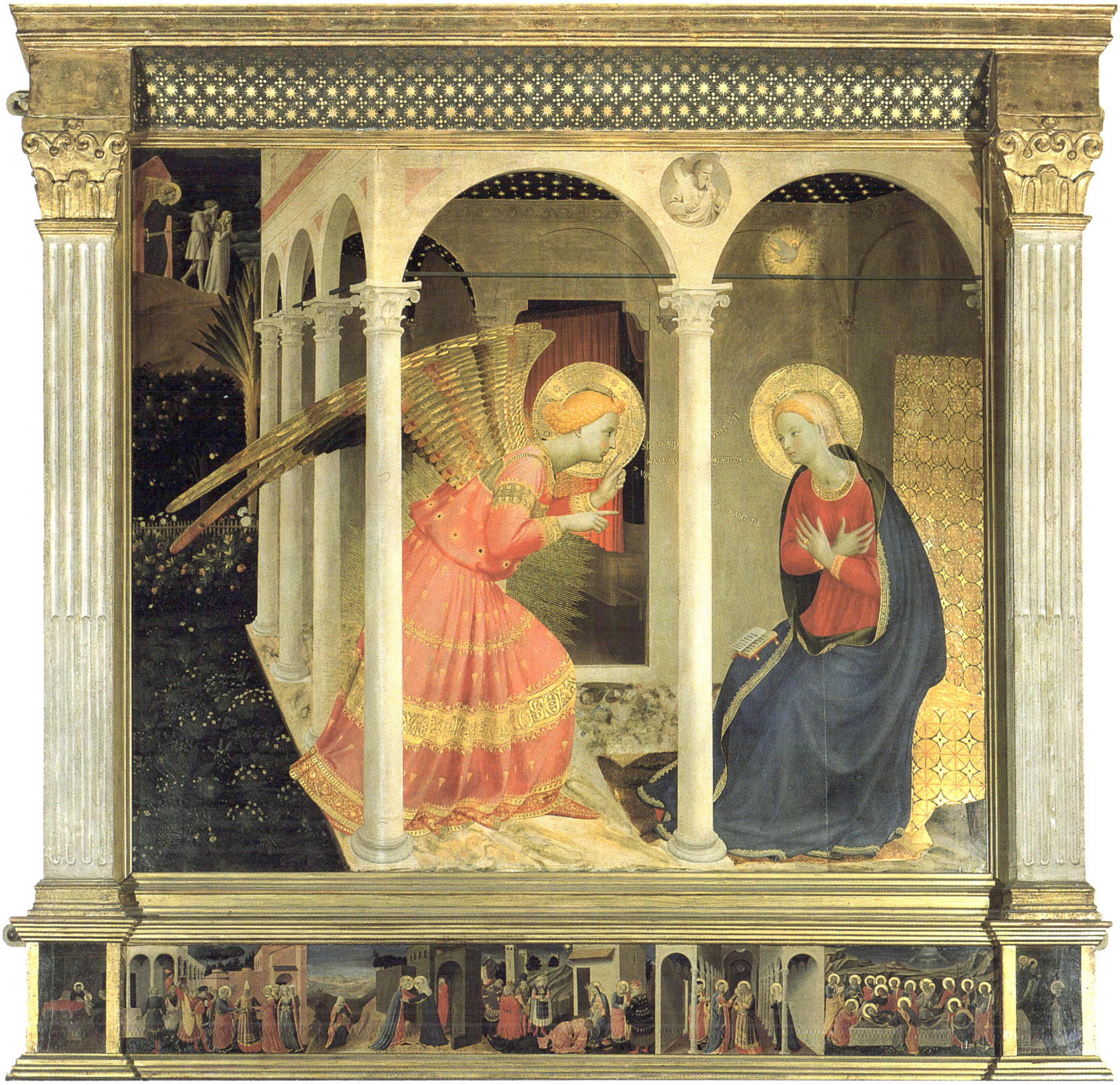

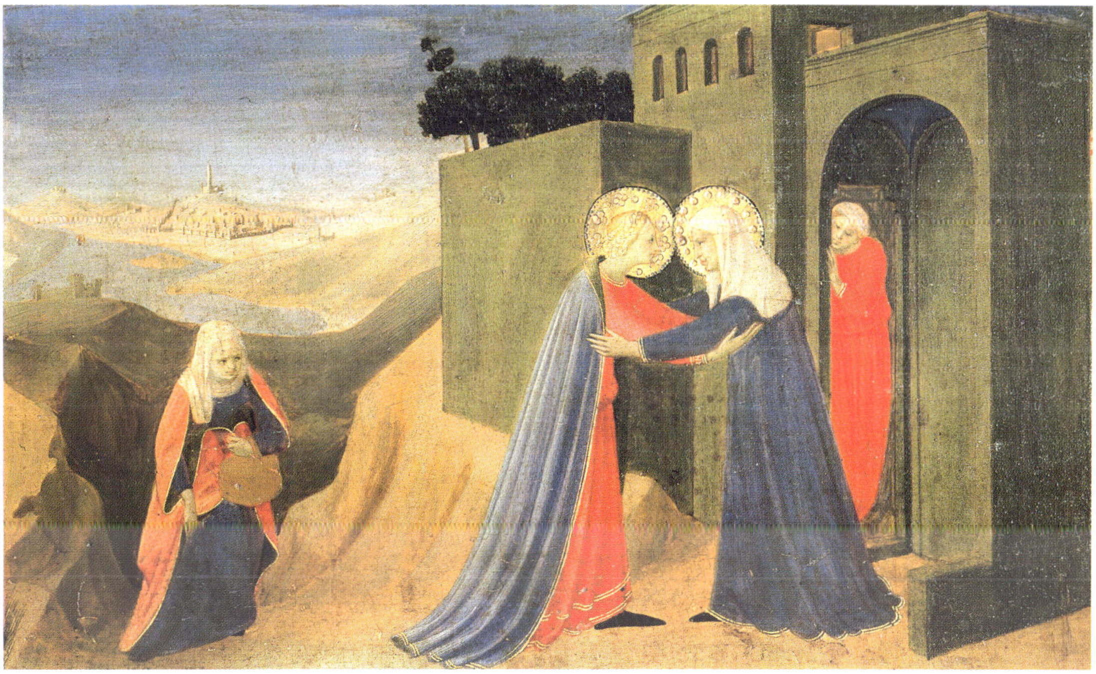

Annunciation,
whole and detail from the predella with the *Visitation*, 1434-1435.
Cortona, Diocese Museum.

Words written in gold express the didactic message of the images. The somber monochrome tones of Adam and Eve contrast with the bright colors of the angel and of Mary, luminous bearers of the message of Redemption.

Linaiuoli, or Linen Drapers' Guild, for a tabernacle, painted both inside and out, for the church of Orsanmichele (see pp. 52-53). The *Tabernacle of the Linen Drapers* presents, framed by a rounded arch, the figure of the Madonna with the Christ Child seated on a broad bench covered with damasked fabric. Splendid, skillfully painted drapery confers on the figure of the Virgin a statuary three-dimensional aspect, while simultaneously offering explicit homage to the patron Guild, which produced fabrics for drapery used to cover altarpieces. Still another reference to the Linen Drapers' Guild may be the gold-colored drapery which, opening at the Virgin's sides like a precious theatrical curtain, allows a glimpse of star-strewn sky at the center of which is the Holy Spirit.

In the episode of the predella with *St Peter preaching in the presence of St Mark*, the choice of the onlookers appears far from casual. The richly dressed group on the right, in fact, represents the city's wealthy upper class, while the women at the center seem intended to portray popular devotion. St Mark is intent on writing his Gospel inspired by the preaching of Peter, assisted by an acolyte holding an ink-well. Two personages in modern dress standing beside him, one with a manuscript, the other in the act of reading a book, symbolize the erudite men of letters, the philologists. The scene, abounding in symbolic figures, and the eloquent iconographic details thus seem to represent the felicitous union between Humanism and religiosity founded on philology, the direct, scrupulous study of the ancient texts. Highly significant and emblematic of the new cultural climate was the intense friendship between the Camaldolensian monk Ambrogio Traversari and the bibliophile and collector of antiquities Niccolò Niccoli. And Niccoli, in fact, allowed Ambrogio Traversari, a scholar of patristics, free use of his magnificent library.

Dating from the middle of the 15th century's fourth decade is the *Annalena Altarpiece* now in the San Marco Museum (see pp. 54-55). This work presents highly innovative features due to its unitary structure, far removed from the polyptych's traditional division into panels. The saints appear grouped at the sides of the Virgin's throne against an architectural background whose space is divided by five rounded arches. The ornamental details are numerous: the inner curve of the arches is decorated with a skillful marble-like effect while a gilded drapery provides a splendid scenic curtain to the Holy Conversation. The same decorative intention may be seen in the refined garland of monochrome leaves and pomegranates adorning the molded frame. To this same period belongs the *Annunciation* now in the Diocese Museum of Cortona, which reiterates the subject and the setting of the similar Madrid painting. Here inscriptions in fine

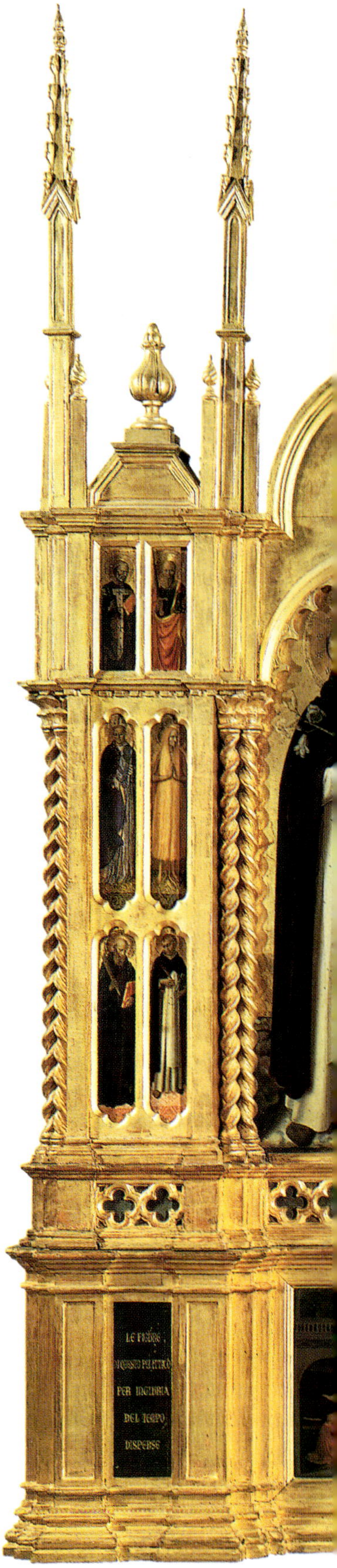

Perugia Polyptych (Madonna and Child with Angels and Sts Dominic, Nicholas of Bari,

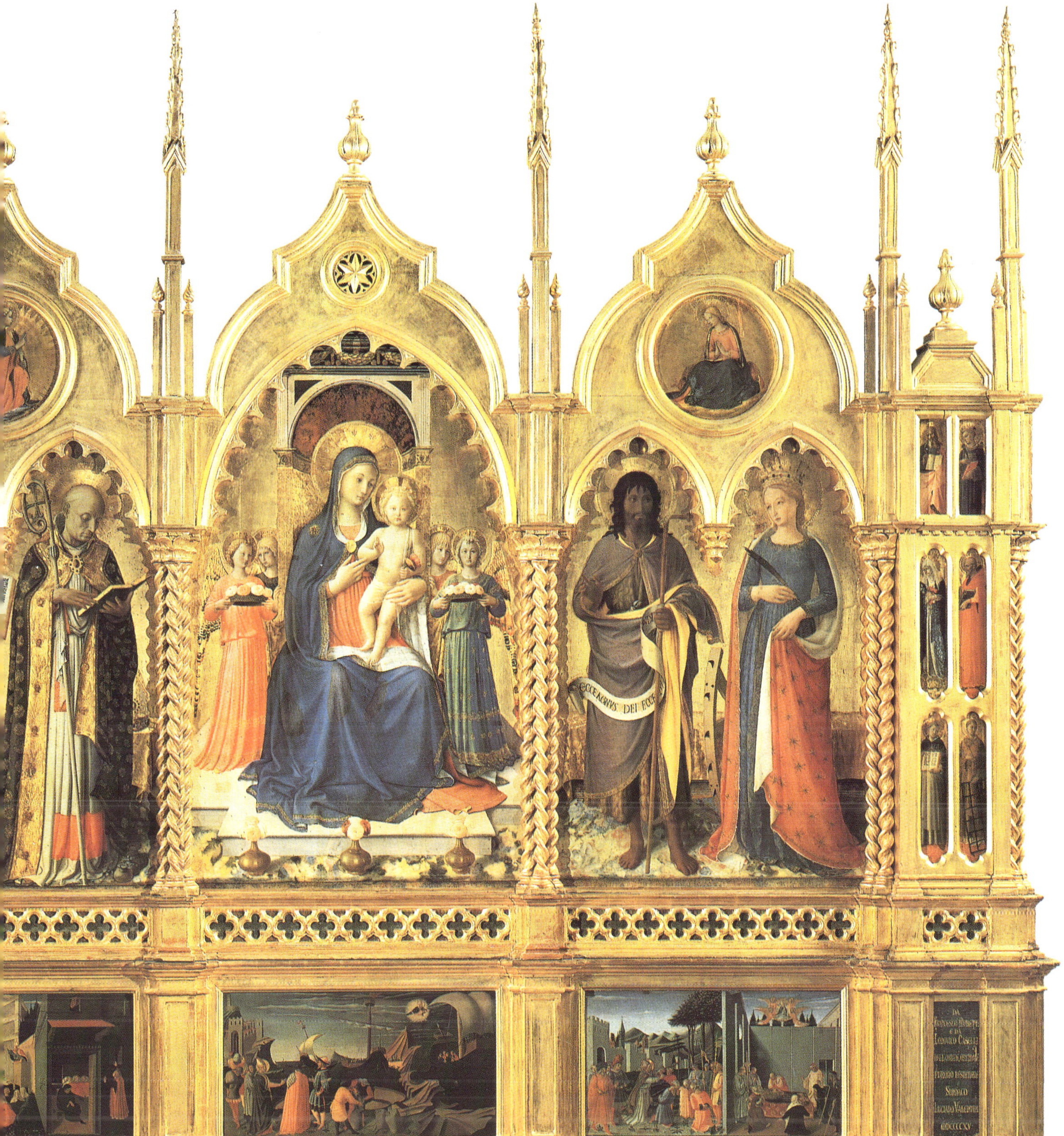

John the Baptist and Catherine of Alexandria), 1437-1438. Perugia, National Gallery of Umbria.

golden characters demonstrate Fra Angelico's interest in the written word, and with it the didactic value of images.

Perhaps dating from 1437-1438, the *Perugia Polyptych*, coming from the chapel of San Nicola in the church of San Domenico at Perugia, returns to the late Gothic form of the triptych. But despite the archaic-style wooden pointed arches on spiral columns, the space in which the scene takes place is unified by the garden, which extends from the Virgin's throne to the side wings, serving as background to the mantles of St Catherine and St Nicholas. Here the perspective scheme is skilled and sure, and great naturalness marks the figures of the angels holding baskets of roses viewed in perfect foreshortening, as well as the figures of St Dominic and St Nicolas of Bari, St John the Baptist and St Catherine. The faces of St Dominic and St Nicolas are intensely characterized, while the colors convey the realistic effect of matter. Moments of pictorial virtuosity can be seen in the clasp on St Nicholas' cope and in the Virgin's star-shaped brooch, in which the central ruby and the pearls surrounding it can be distinguished. In the book held up by St Dominic can be read some verses taken from the Second Epistle of St Paul to Timothy, testifying to the painter's analytic skill while reiterating once again his constant interest in the written word. Details rendered with such care have suggested that Fra Angelico may have had some contact with Flemish painting and elaborated his own personal view of it, although how this may have happened is unknown. Information on the existence of a dense network of commercial relations between Florentine merchants and bankers and the country of Flanders is however abundant. It has also been hypothesized that the strongly characterized features of St Nicholas may represent those of Pope Eugene IV, who had shown vivid interest in the Dominican community at Perugia. At the time the Pope was residing in the monastery of Santa Maria Novella, where he may have already established with Fra Angelico that relationship destined to assume great importance in the San Marco years. Conversely, it has been suggested that the face of St Nicholas may be that of Nicholas V, the Humanist Tommaso Parentucelli, who had been the librarian of San Marco during the same years when Fra Angelico was frescoing the cells.

Dating from the second half of the fourth decade is the *Lament for the Dead Christ* now in the San Marco Museum but coming from the Compagnia di Santa Croce al Tempio. The work had been commissioned by Fra Sebastiano Benintendi, who wanted it to represent one of his ancestors, the Blessed Villana (died in 1360). On the border of the Virgin's mantle the date 1440 indicates the year in which the work was probably completed, while the phrase in the vulgar tongue XR[IST]O YH[ES]V LAMOR MIO CRVCIFISSO ("Jesus Christ my love crucified") pronounced by the Blessed Villana has a didactic function in expressing her devotion to the cross. The atmospheric expedient of the sunset light emphasizes the sorrow of this episode from the Gospels, treated by the Friar in the elegiac tones of a devout, composed contemplation of the holy drama.

Lament for the Dead Christ, whole and details, 1436-1440. Florence, San Marco Museum.

This work was painted for the church of Santa Croce al Tempio near the Arno River and the walls of the city. Here prisoners condemned to death spent their last hours before execution, which usually took place outside of the city walls. The subject of the work was particularly appropriate, since those who were soon to face death could reflect here on the mystic aspects linked to the Passion of Christ. An almost Flemish care for detail appears in the treatment of the gem-studded crown worn by St Catherine of Alexandria who, kneeling beside the Blessed Villana, witnesses, mournful and absorbed, the Deposition.

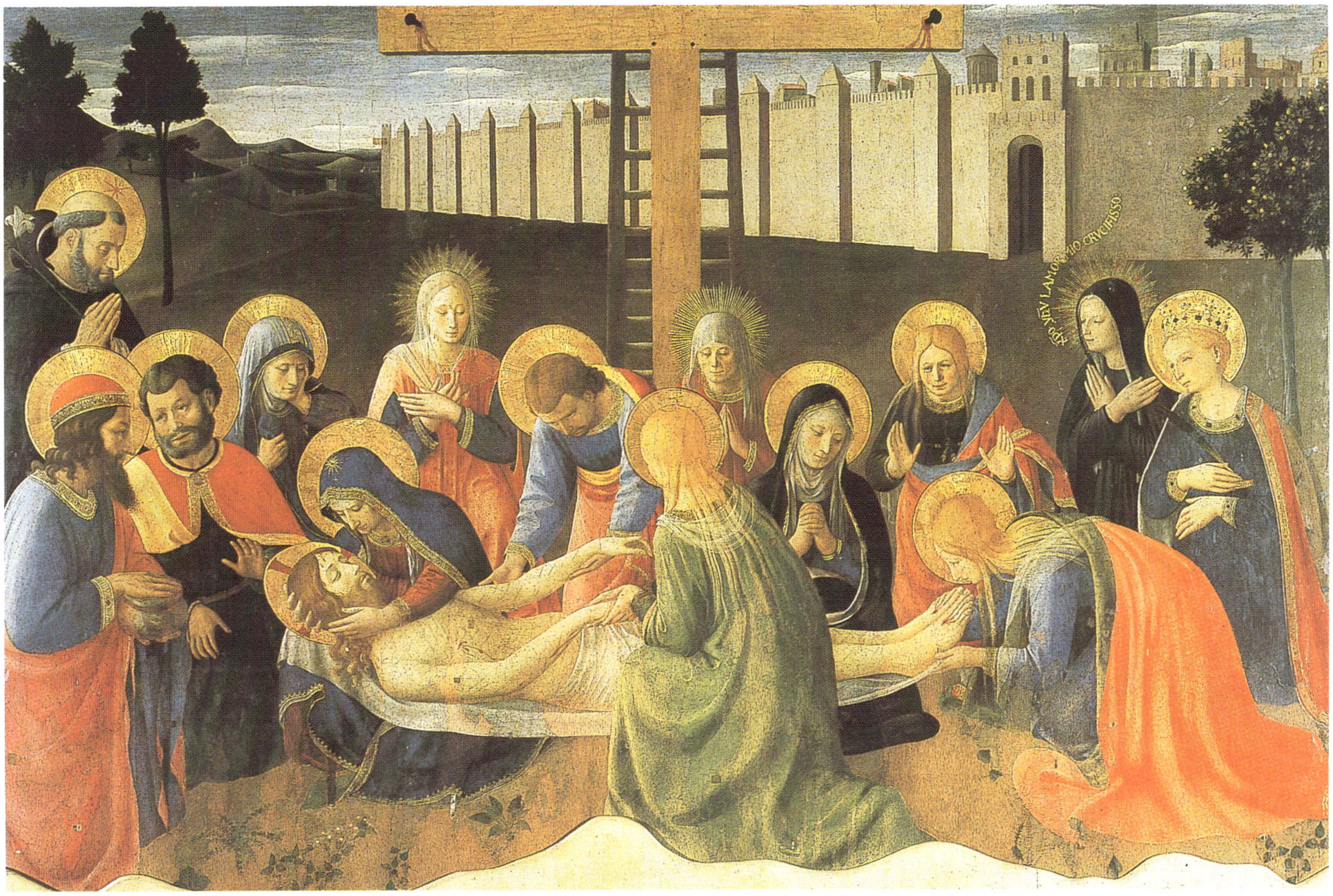

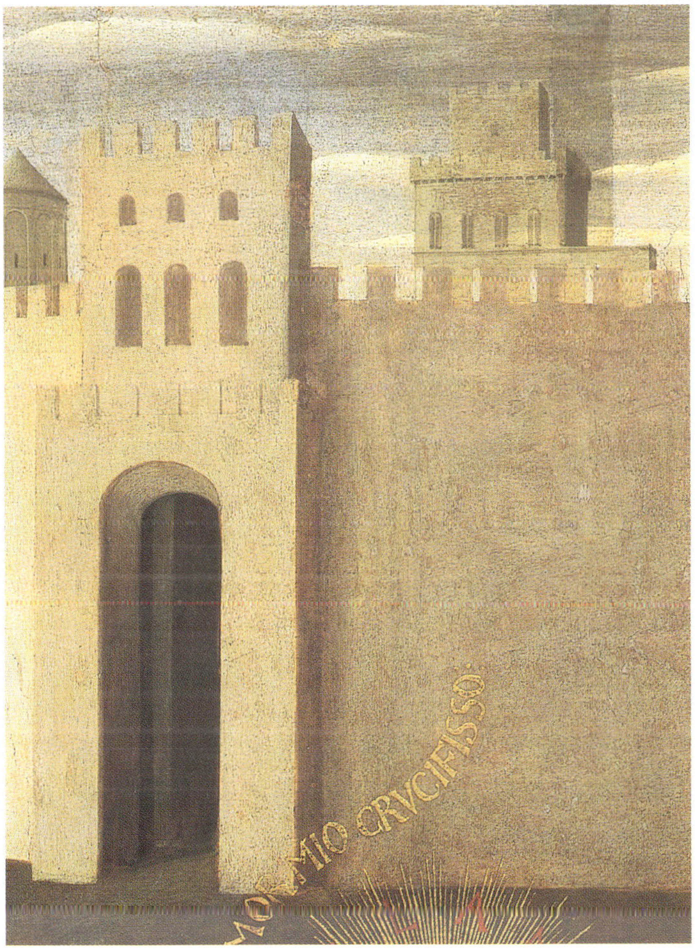
MIO CRVCIFISSO

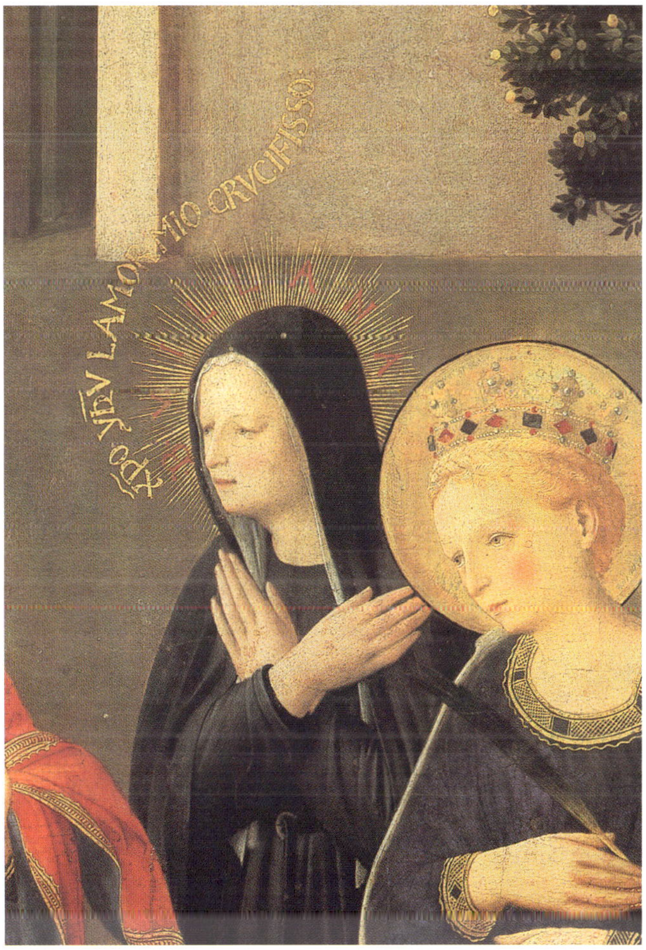
XPO YEV LAMO
MIO CRVCIFISSO

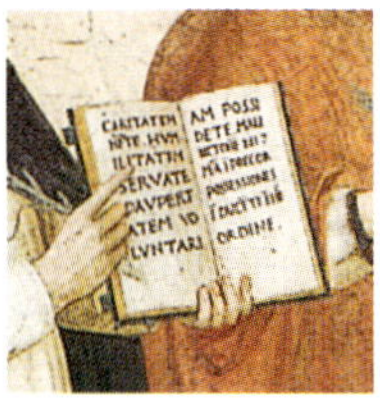

The San Marco frescoes

For Florentine history as well as for the artistic career of Fra Angelico, 1434 was a crucial year. It was in that year, in fact, that Cosimo the Elder returned in triumph to the city, after a brief period of exile. Political mistakes had broken up the party of the city's oligarchy, opposed to the Medici family, so that Cosimo was allowed to return with joy to his residence in Via Larga and to begin an inexorable rise to power. Cosimo, an able politician, soon managed to procure for himself a vast following, due to the wise, well-balanced conduct that earned him the epithet of *pater patriae*, "father of his country". Influenced by the preaching of Antonino Pierozzi, Cosimo became a sustainer of the cause of the Dominican Observance, a powerful order that could boast outstanding preachers as well as sympathy and support from the highest ecclesiastical spheres. In 1436 a bull proclaimed by Pope Eugene IV stipulated that the monastery of San Marco, a decaying structure inhabited by a few Sylvestrine monks, would pass under the jurisdiction of the Observant Dominicans in the monastery at Fiesole. San Marco was located at a crucial point in the city, very close to the important church of the Santissima Annunziata and not far from the cathedral of Santa Maria del Fiore and from Palazzo Medici in Via Larga. This strategic location, the care of the Dominican order and the interest of Cosimo the Elder, personally involved in financing the restoration of the buildings, could not fail to confer on the monastery a central role in the political-religious life of the city. Cosimo's intervention was based on sincere devotion, not devoid of the desire to manifest his "virtù" to the city of which he was the occult lord. Accordingly, he ensured that the church too was renovated and endowed with an altarpiece painted by Fra Angelico to adorn the high altar. A few years later San Marco was given an elegant library, again at the desire of Cosimo, designed by Michelozzo to house, along with other precious volumes, the wealth of Greek and Latin classical texts it had received at the death of Niccolò Niccoli.

Annunciation, c. 1440. Florence, San Marco Museum, corridor of the first floor.

The elaborate classical capitals and the volumes of the columns make the portico in which the Annunciation takes place realistically convincing. As compared to other versions of the same subject, the composition is simplified and the mystic atmosphere is more intense. Adam and Eve are absent while the scene, dominated only by the figures of the angel and the Virgin, is framed in an architectural setting that recalls the structure of Michelozzo's library within the monastery, located very near to Fra Angelico's *Annunciation*.

The architectural structure of the San Marco building complex possessed the characteristics necessary to meet the needs of the order: a church in which to celebrate mass each day and welcome the faithful who flocked to hear the preachers, and a monastery in which to live and study. A cycle of frescoes on the walls extending from the Chapter House and the corridors to the cells would fulfill the purposes of both moral exhortation and stimulus to meditation. The Prior of the monastery had been, since 1439, Antonino Pierozzi, a leading figure in religious Humanism, convinced of the importance of the figurative arts for the scope of divine contemplation, and supporter of Fra Angelico as the artist best-qualified to translate the order's theological principles into painting. It may have been Antonino himself to suggest to Fra

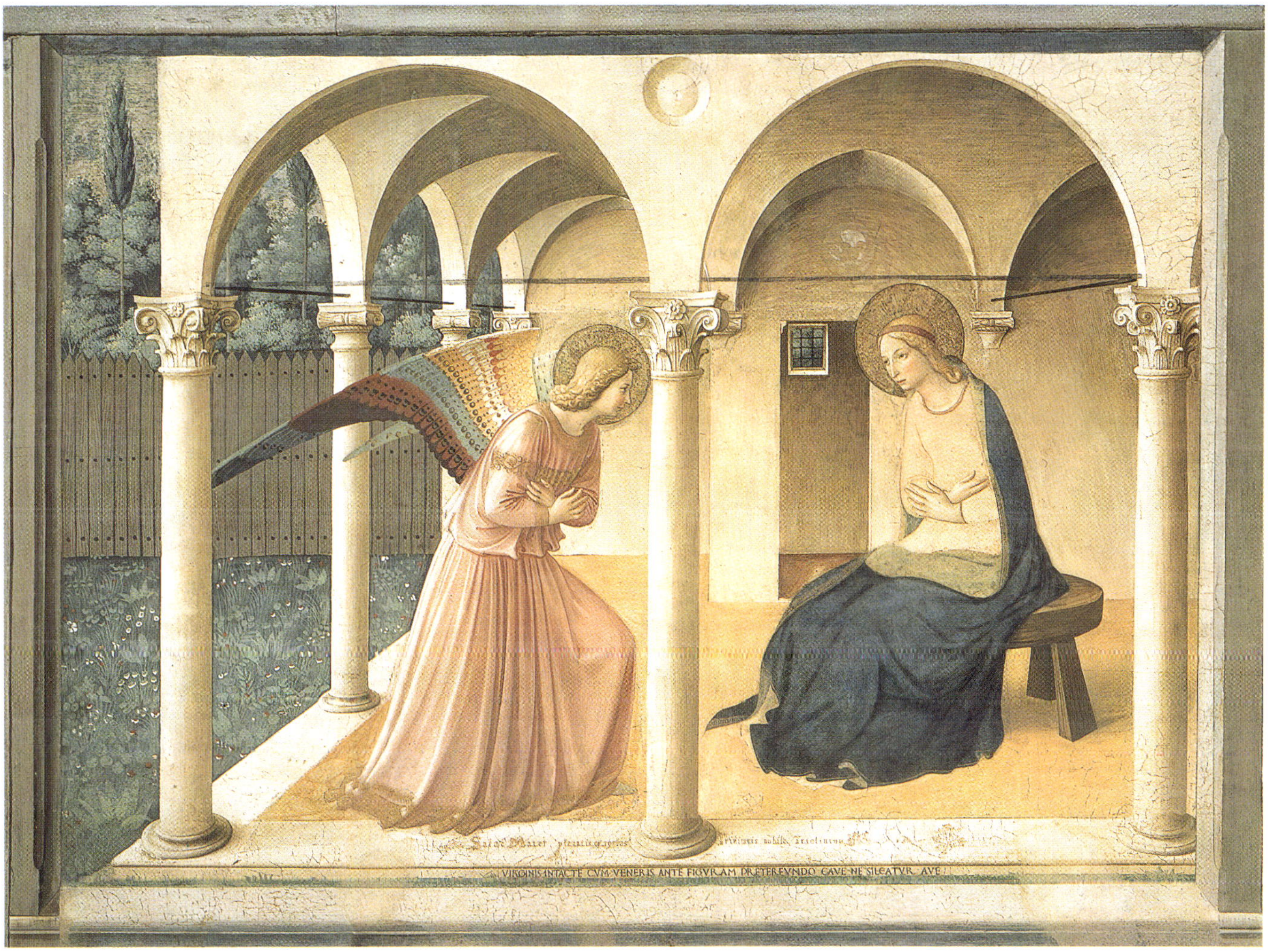

Angelico the concepts to be illustrated in the cycle of paintings, completed with the aid of assistants in a relatively brief span of time, between 1439 and 1445. In spite of the participation of numerous hands, including those of the young Benozzo Gozzoli, critics have noted the substantial conceptual, programmatic and stylistic unity of the entire pictorial cycle. What makes the San Marco undertaking a case unique in art history is without doubt the innovative concept of collocating some of the frescoes in the cells of the monks, when fresco painting was instead generally reserved to zones of common use, such as the chapter house and the refectory.

In the first cloister, accessible also to non-ecclesiastics, Fra Angelico painted *St Dominic adoring the Crucifix*, a true manifesto of Dominican faith; in two of the five lunettes the images of *The Dead Christ* and *Christ as Pilgrim with Two Dominicans*, and in the other three the saints Dominic, Peter the Martyr and Thomas, dear to the order.

The Chapter House, frescoed by August 1442, the date on which the first official meeting was held here, presents a majestic *Crucifixion*. The painter thus placed the cardinal event of the Christian faith at the center of the monks' devoted contemplation. The faces of the personages represented are strongly characterized, and their gestures appear noble, perhaps inspired by the classical examples extolled by Humanism. In this place, where guests and important visitors were received, the frescoes were designed to fulfill the purpose of illustrating with decorous eloquence the prestige of the order and its doctrinaire principles. Most of the frescoes are located on the upper floor of the monastery, along the corridors and in the cells. Fra Angelico and his assistants painted here forty-six images, dis-

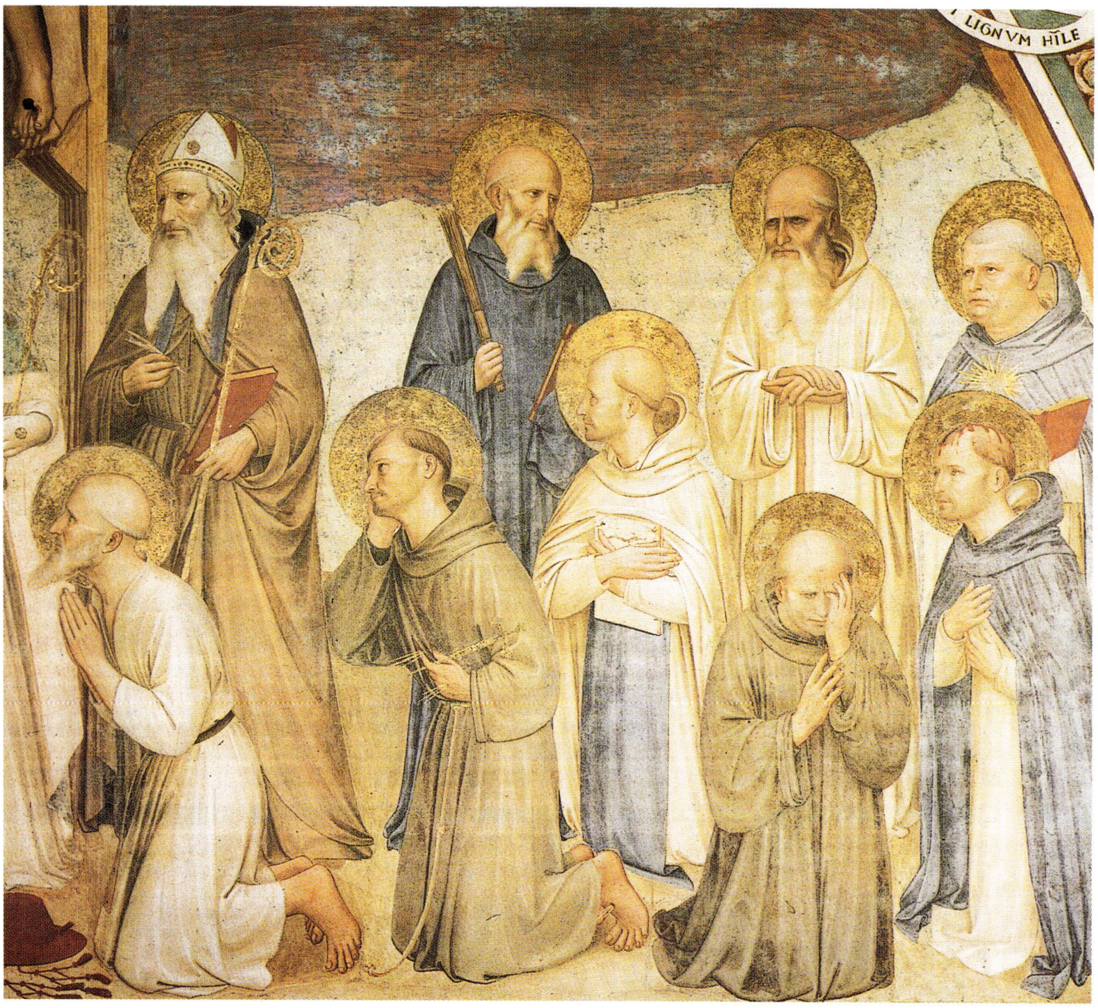

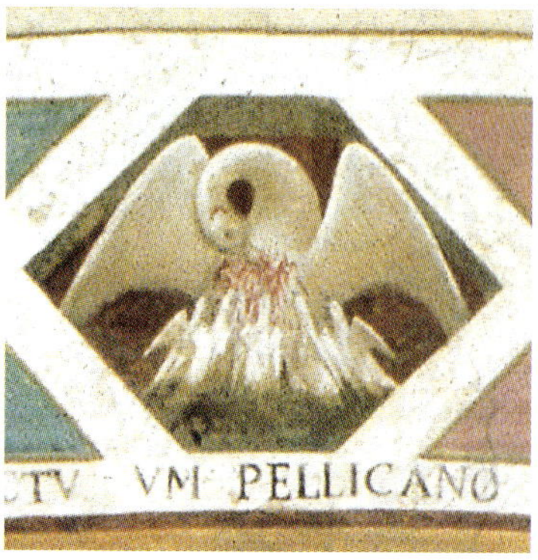

Crucifixion, whole and details, c. 1442. Florence, San Marco Museum, Chapter House.

Recognizable among the personages gathered to worship the Cross are, at right, the saints of the Dominican order along with the Doctors of the church and founders of religious orders, leading figures in the

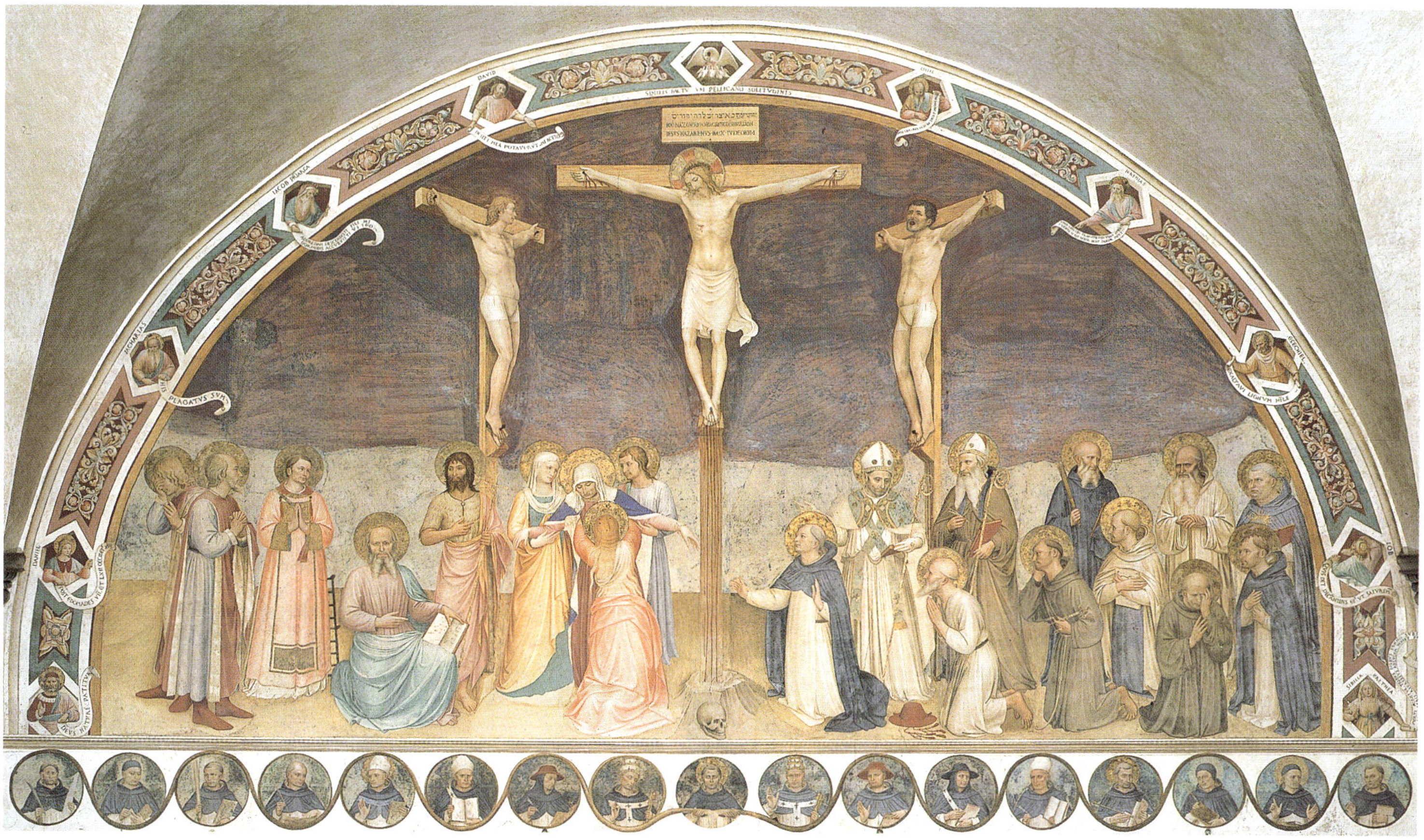

ecclesiastical history which started with the Crucifixion. On the left are instead the saints linked to the Medici family, the patron saints (Lawrence, Cosmas and Damian), recognizable by their iconographic attributes. In the medallions on the band below the scene appears a line of Dominican saints and Blessed ones, while from the upper frame look out nine prophets as well as the Eritrean Sibyl and an unidentified personage, the figures who prophesied the death of Christ and the ensuing Redemption, reiterated by the image of the pelican (at center), symbol of the Messiah's sacrifice.

tributed among the forty-four cells of the northern dormitory, which may have been used for non-ecclesiastical guests, the eastern one, occupied by the clergy, and the southern one, reserved to novices. A double cell, at the far western end of the northern dormitory, was destined to the private use of Cosimo the Elder, benefactor of the monastery, and was frescoed with an *Adoration of the Magi* (see pp. 58-59).

It is possible that the frescoes, organized according to a generic iconographical program, were designed to illustrate the general principles of the order without any particular attention to those who would benefit by the images painted in the cells. But art historians have shown how their succession does not coincide at all with the traditional sequence of events in the life of Christ, thus making plausible the hypothesis that behind such an original narration of the Evangelical message and behind the substantial difference in tone and in iconographical selection of images, there was in reality a complex intention. The different destination of the cells, then, occupied by laymen and monks of different ranking in the hierarchy of the order (novices and clerics), has suggested that each image conceived by Fra Angelico was destined to a particular member of the monastic community on the basis of his own theological knowledge. The literary references forming the basis for the program may have been the writings of the Pseudo-Dioniges Areopagite, known to Fra Angelico through the mediation of men of learning

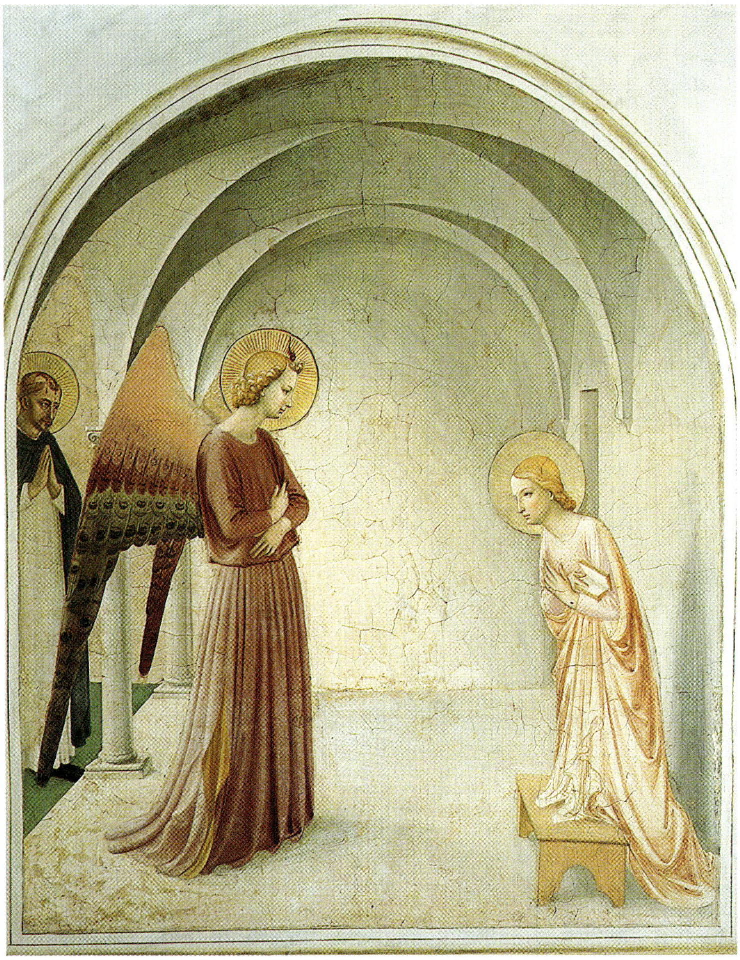

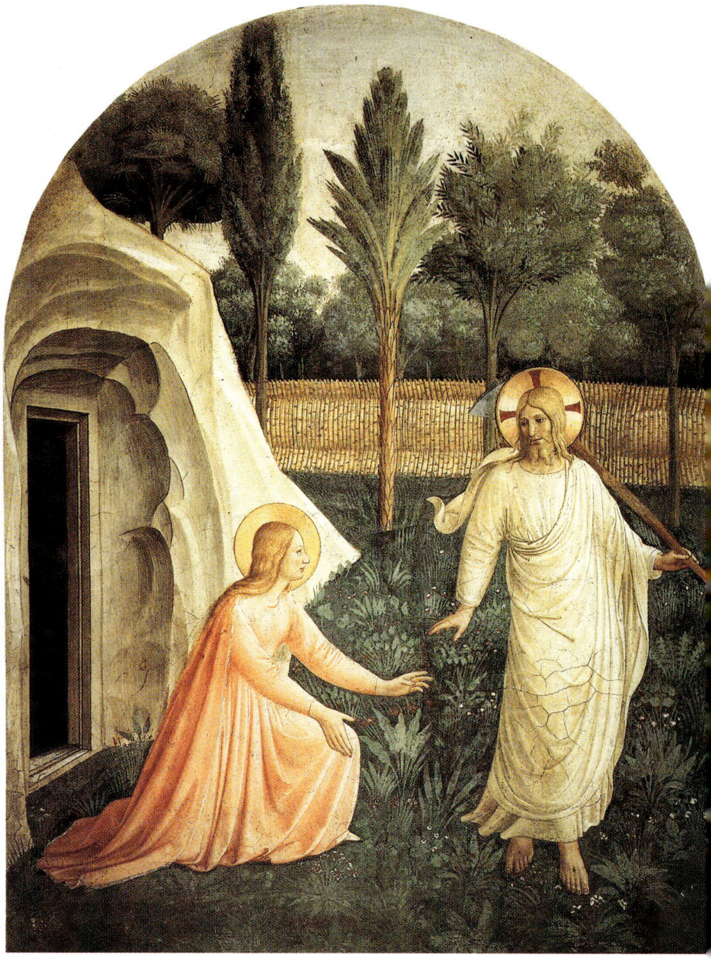

Annunciation, 1438-1443. Florence, San Marco Museum, cell 3.

Noli me tangere, 1438-1443. Florence, San Marco Museum, cell 1.

such as Ambrogio Traversari, Tommaso Parentucelli and Antonino Pierozzi. According to this hypothesis, the division of Fra Angelico's frescoes among three groups of cells coincides with three categories of the clergy, distinguished according to their level of knowledge of the Christian mysteries theorized by the Areopagite. The three initiatory stages would thus correspond to the principles of purification, enlightenment and perfection, according to the concept of a progressive detachment of the spirit from matter. To the novices then, who were limited to obeying and listening without taking part in religious activities, were destined cells 15-21 in the southern dormitory. In each of these cells appears the image, easily read, of the *Crucifix*.

The double cell 10-11, located at the intersection between the southern and eastern dormitories, has been identified as that of the Prior on the basis of the subjects represented. Here the theme of the purification of the Virgin, the central figure in the *Presentation of Jesus in the Temple*, was intended to induce meditation, while in the other chamber of the Prior's cell the holy conversation with the emblematic presences of St Augustine and St Thomas, who holds the sacred book, recalls the importance of the rule and of doctrine in the instruction of novices. Cells 22-29, destined to the clerics, appear centered around Christ's Passion and his sacrifice, themes

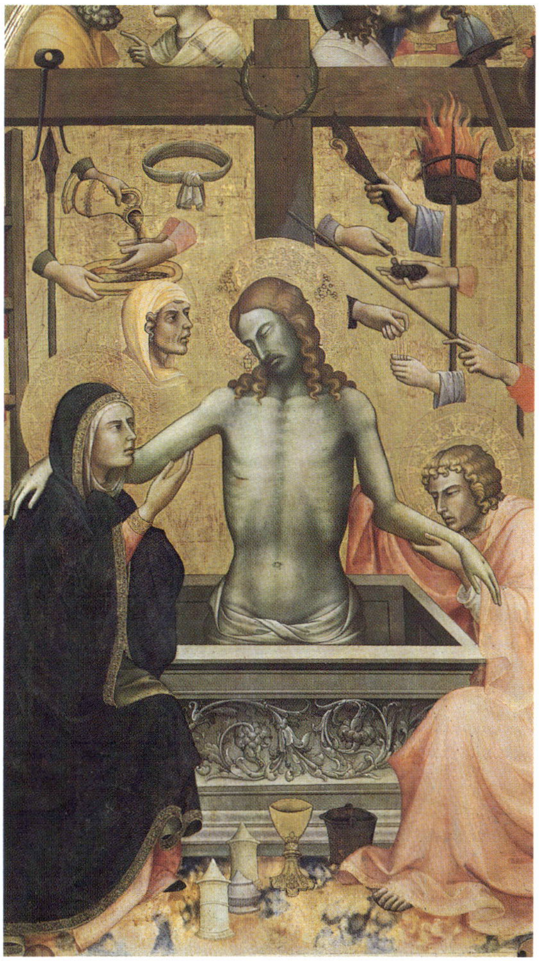

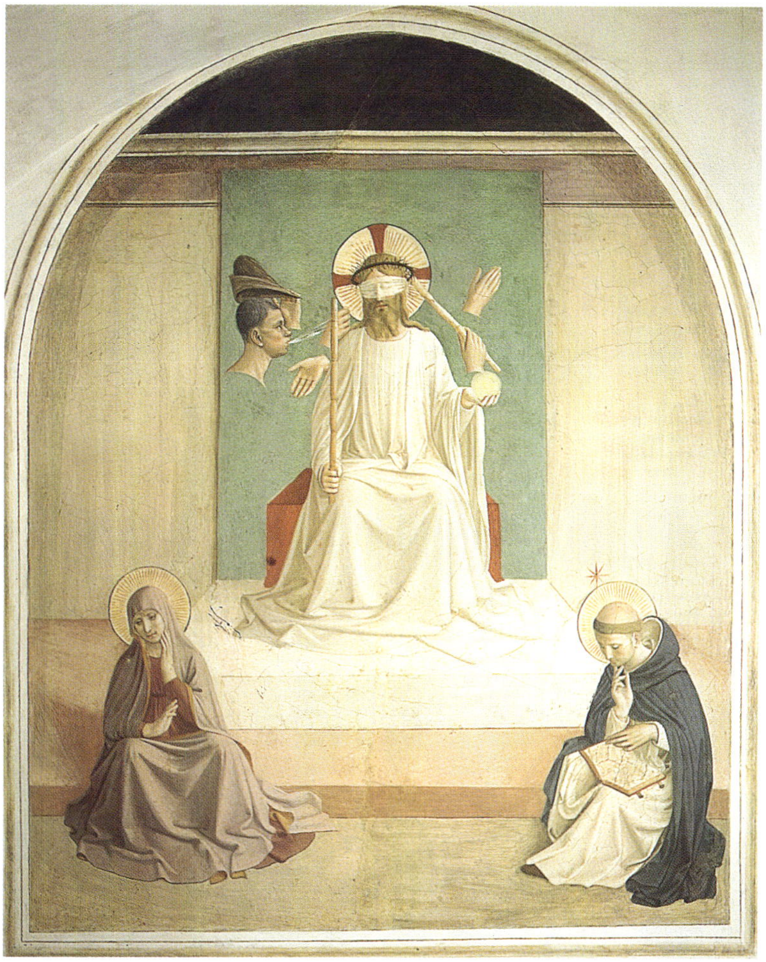

Pietà by Lorenzo Monaco, now at the Accademia Gallery, Florence, c. 1405.

The Mocking of Christ, 1438 1443. Florence, San Marco Museum, cell 7.

of greater profundity. The frescoed images, in accordance with the writings of the Areopagite, would thus correspond to the second stage, that of enlightenment. They are: *Christ crucified with the Virgin, Christ crucified with the Virgin and St Thomas, The Baptism of Christ, Christ crucified with the Virgin, St Mary Magdalene and St Dominic, Christ in the tomb, Christ at the column, Christ carrying the Cross, Crucifixion with St Peter the Martyr.*

Cells 1-9, highly original as compared to the others, would according to this interpretation illustrate the third stage of Dionysian progress: perfection considered to be contemplation of the divine. The complex iconographic program, synthesizing the fundamental mysteries of the story of salvation, would thus present again the themes, already dealt with, of Christ's Passion and his death, but with the aim of portraying the mystic concepts of the Incarnation and Resurrection. The events depicted here – *Noli me tangere, Lament for the Dead Christ, Annunciation, Crucifixion, Nativity, Transfiguration, The Mocking of Christ, The Maries at the tomb* and the *Coronation of the Virgin* – seem arranged according to the rhythmic sequence: Resurrection, Passion, Incarnation; Passion, Incarnation, Resurrection; Passion, Resurrection, union with God. The frescoes are distinguished by a sublime tone, by a rigorous perspective scheme and by a synthetic language rich in in-

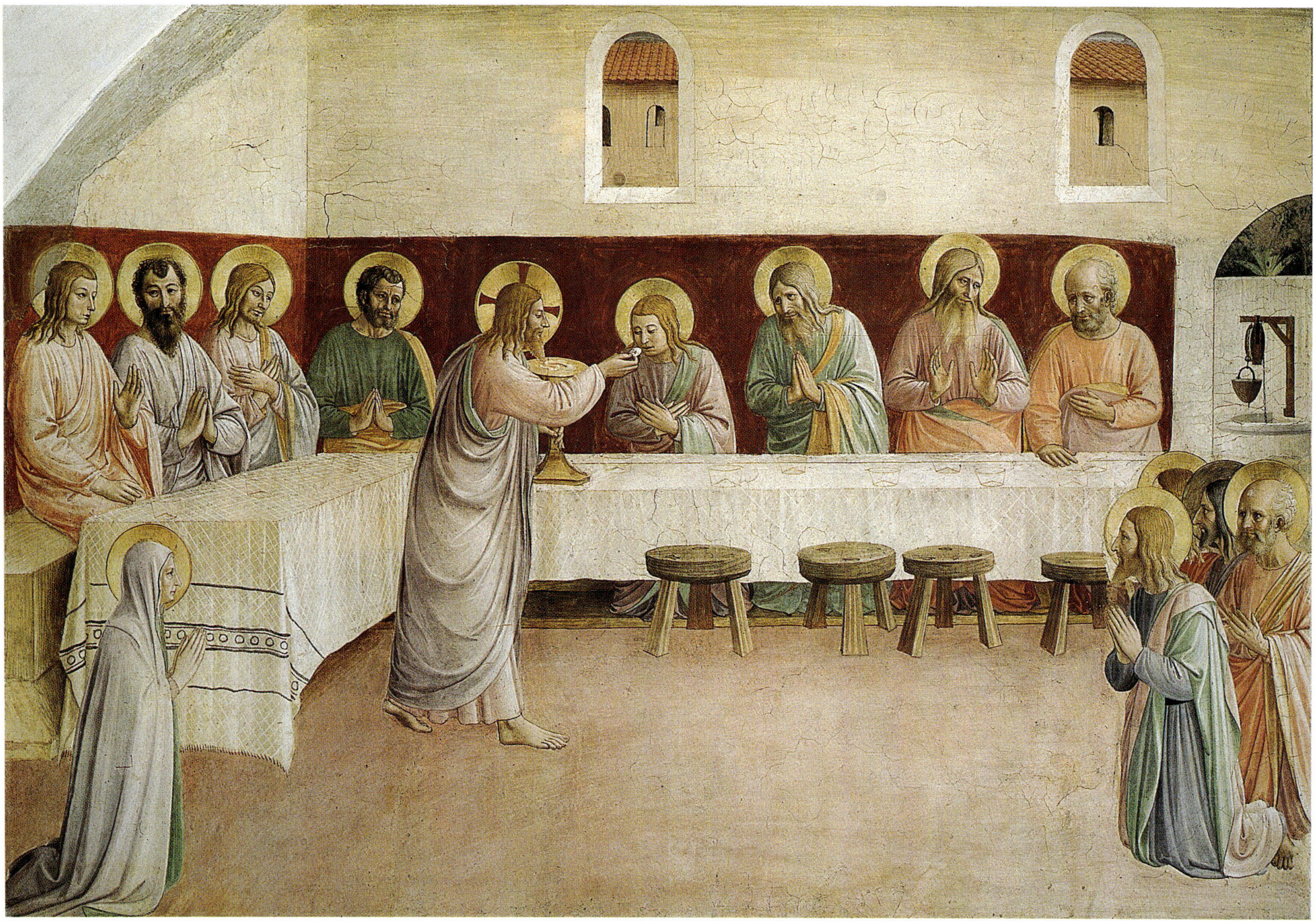

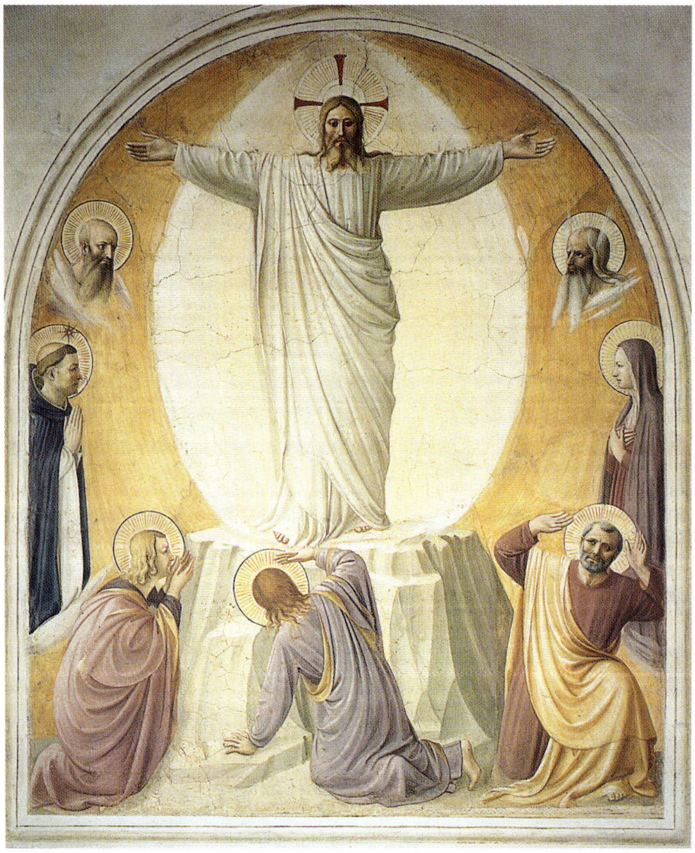

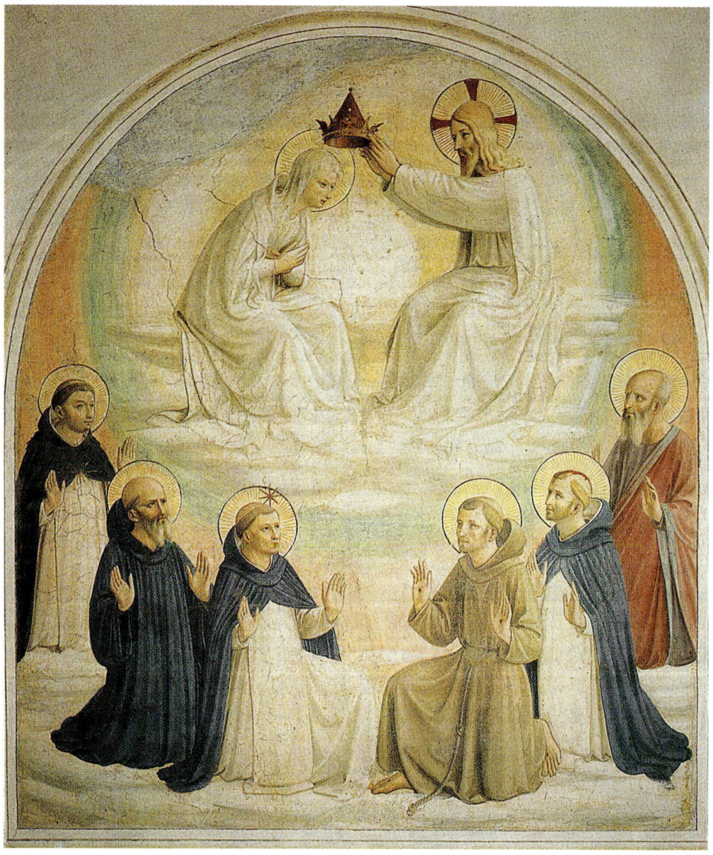

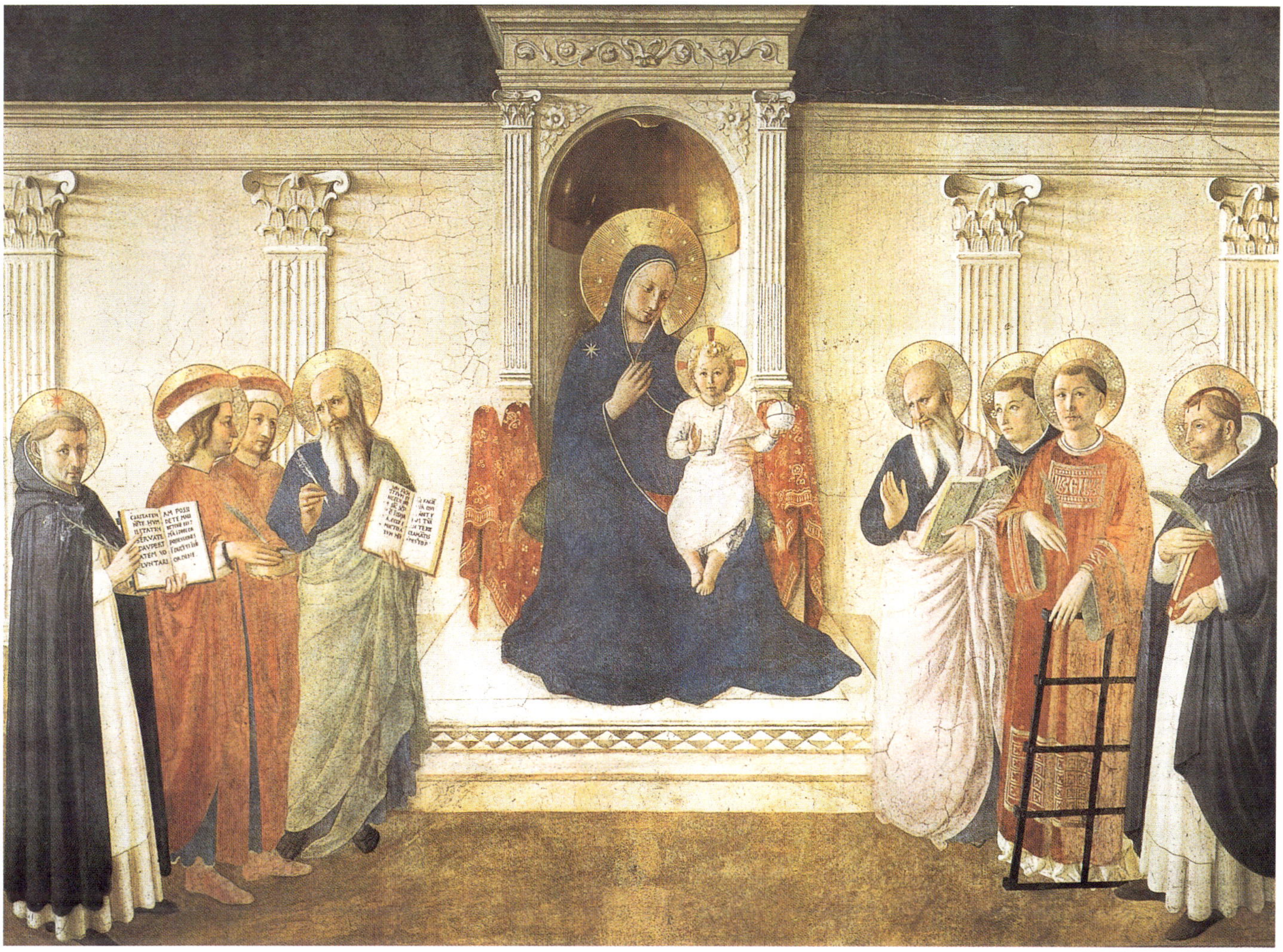

Virgin of the Shadows (Madonna and Child with Sts Dominic, Cosmas and Damian, Mark, John the Evangelist, Thomas, Lawrence and Peter the Martyr), c. 1443. Florence, San Marco Museum, corridor of the first floor.

At left: *Institution of the Eucharist, Transfiguration* and *Coronation of the Virgin*, 1438-1443. Florence, San Marco Museum, cells 35, 6 and 9.

tensely symbolic words. Particularly emblematic is *The Mocking of Christ*, in which the Passion, in an atmosphere of intense meditation, takes on metaphysical tones through the archaic-style expedient of suspending the symbols of the Passion around the central figure of the blindfolded Christ.

In the corridors three different frescoes illustrate the *Annunciation*, a recurrent subject in the monastery, the *Christ on the Cross with St Dominic* and a holy conversation with Sts Dominic, Cosmas, Damian, Mark, John the Evangelist, Thomas Aquinas, Lawrence and Peter the Martyr, evocatively called the *Madonna of the Shadows*. The work owes its name to a singular pictorial expedient, the play of shadows projected onto the wall by the Corinthian capitals, painted in accordance with the direction of the real source of light coming from the end of the corridor.

The entire monastic complex and the church, endowed with a magnificent new altarpiece by Fra Angelico, were solemnly consecrated on the day of the Epiphany of 1443, in the presence of Pope Eugene IV. On that occasion the Pope was housed in the cell of Cosimo the Elder, where the fresco of the *Adoration of the Magi* was to become a painted memorial to that crucially important day in the history of the monastery.

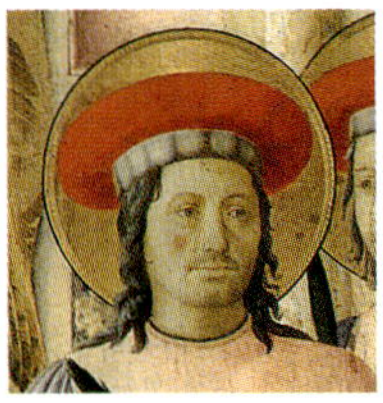

The Niccolina Chapel and the last works

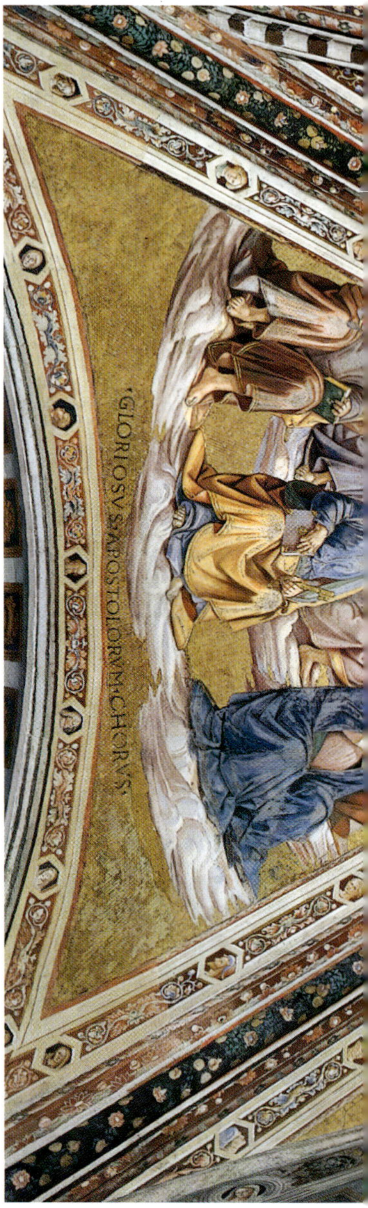

While Fra Angelico was beginning his work in San Marco, in 1439, there took place a very significant event for the religious spheres of Florence: the Council that proposed to reunite the Western and the Eastern churches in a higher ecumenical ideal was held. On the occasion of the Council, presided over by Pope Eugene IV, there converged on the city the highest authorities of the two Churches and with them philosophers and men of learning, scholars of the ancient texts written by the Fathers of the Church and the philosophical works of Greek and Latin antiquity. The city of Florence was the ideal setting for this encounter. Already since the beginning of the century Humanists such as Coluccio Salutati, Leonardo Bruni and Niccolò Niccoli had dedicated themselves to studying the ancient authors and collecting their works, debating the contents with leading figures from the ecclesiastical world such as Ambrogio Traversari, head of the Camaldolensian order, and Antonino Pierozzi, Prior of the monastery of San Marco starting from the same year in which the Council was held.

In his will Niccoli had left the monastery of his friend Traversari his precious collection of Greek and Latin classics, but when Traversari became the head of the order, he complied with the desire of Cosimo the Elder, that the volumes should go to form the basic nucleus of the San Marco library. As soon as the construction of the library hall was completed, in 1444, it was Cosimo himself to entrust the preparation of the plan and its implementation to Cardinal Parentucelli, an outstanding figure in religious Humanism who was some years later to become Pope under the name of Nicholas V. The cardinal had arrived in Florence a few years ago, residing there occasionally up to the time of the Council, when he settled there definitively to take part in the debates. It was on that occasion that Parentucelli met Fra Angelico who, after having completed the undertaking of frescoing San Marco, was to join the Cardinal in Rome to decorate with frescoes

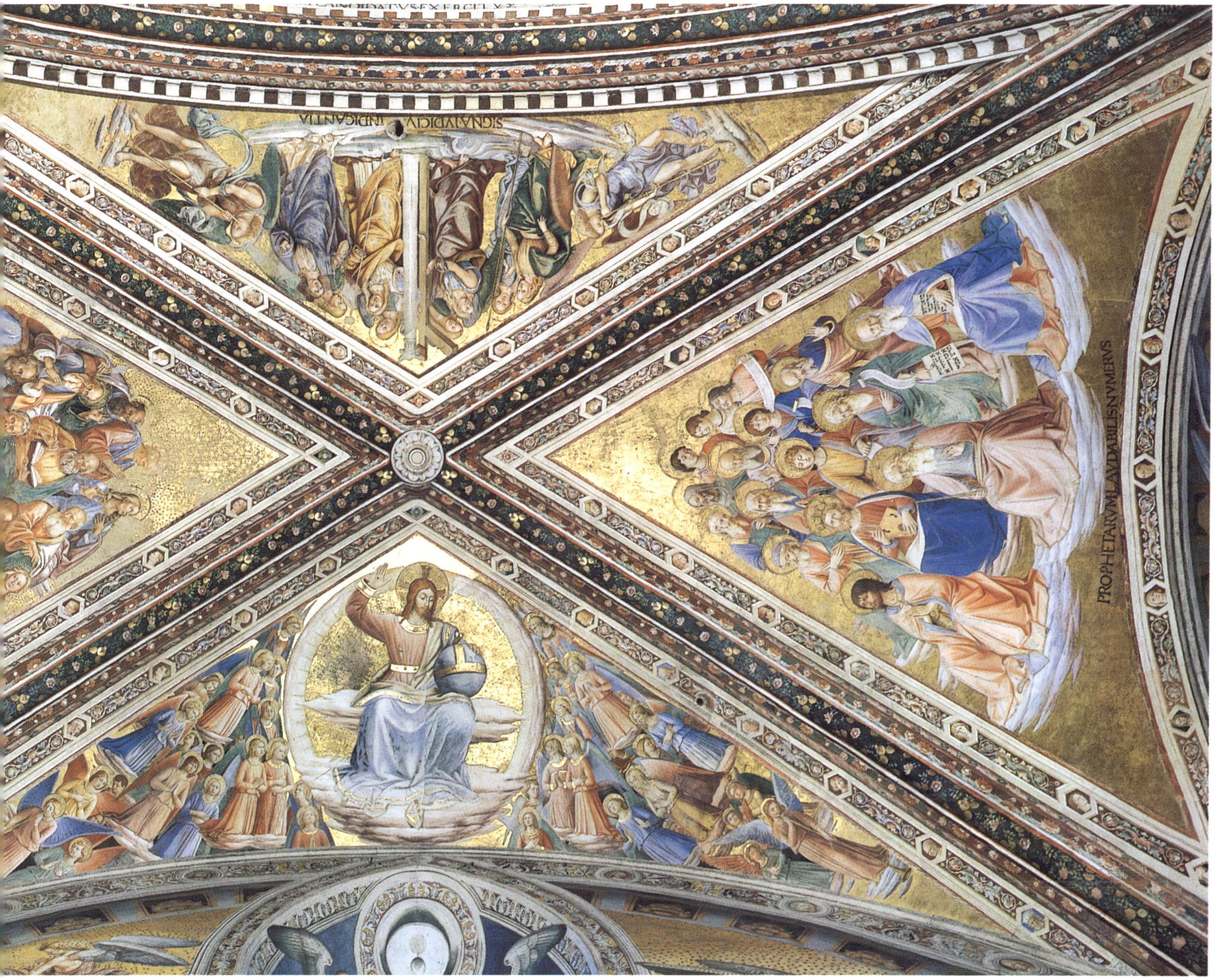

Ceiling of the San Brizio Chapel, 1447. Orvieto, Duomo.

In the summer of 1447 Fra Angelico and his assistants, among them the young Benozzo Gozzoli, frescoed the vaulting cell with *Christ the Judge and Angels* and the one with *Sixteen Prophets*. The ceiling was completed by Luca Signorelli years later, between 1499 and 1502.

his personal chapel. Art historians have noted how already Eugene IV, present at San Marco in 1443, was an admirer of the painter and the probable client, in Rome, for some now lost works by Fra Angelico.

But when did Fra Angelico go to Rome for the first time? A document certifies that in 1445 he was still at San Marco while in May of 1446 his presence is mentioned in Rome, where he had been summoned by Pope Eugene IV, perhaps already some time ago. Engaged in carrying out the Pope's commissions, Fra Angelico seems to have left Rome only in the summer of 1447, when he began to fresco the chapel of San Brizio in the Duomo of Orvieto. Of the artist's numerous Roman works, only the Niccolina Chapel seems to have survived. The client of the Vatican undertaking, Nicholas V, had dedicated himself from the beginning of his papacy to the construction of a great library, for which he sought rare and precious books all over Europe. Around the Pope gathered the leading figures of Human-

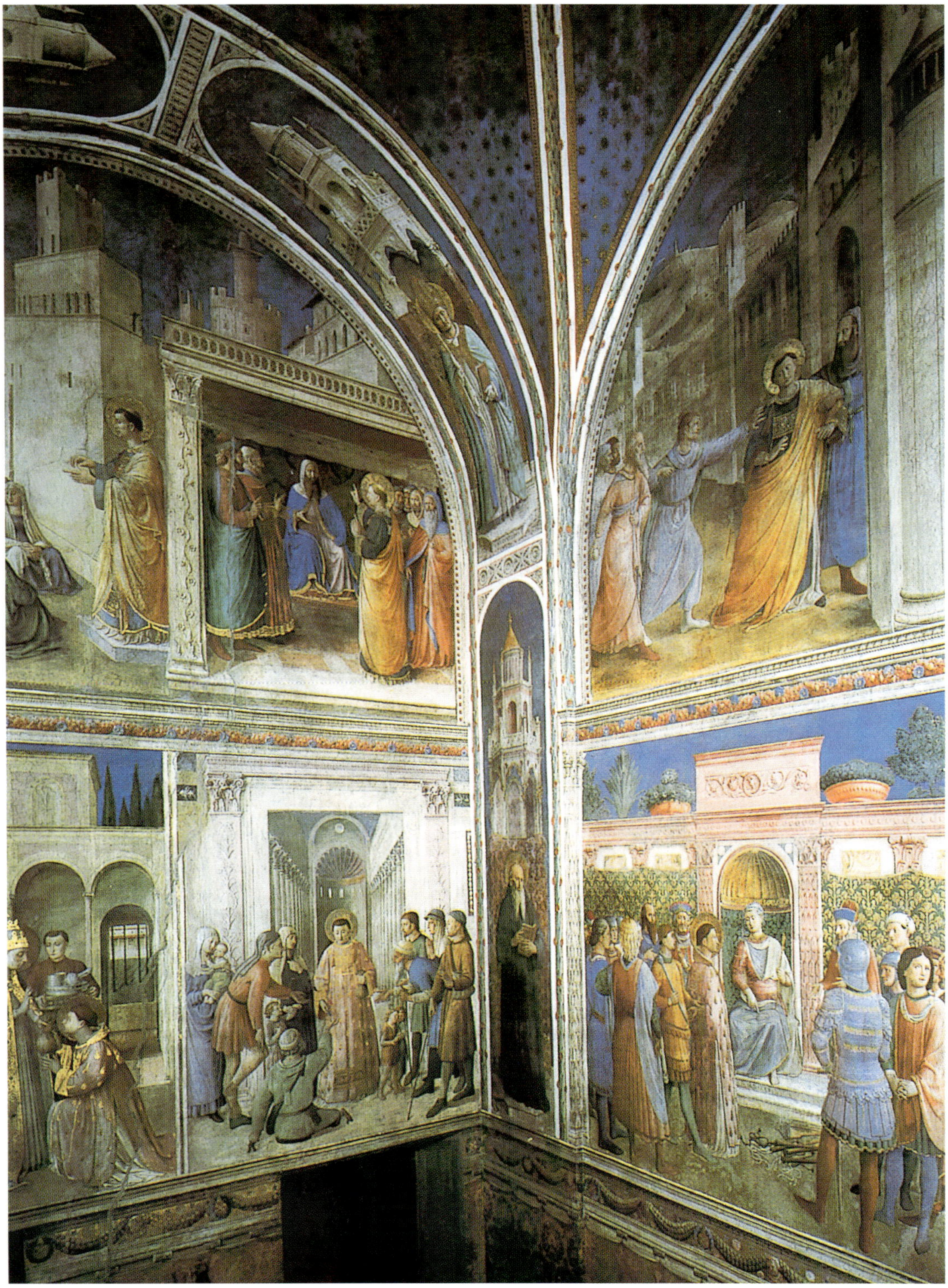

View of the frescoes in the Niccolina Chapel, 1448-1449. Vatican City, Vatican Palaces.

The chapel served as place of private prayer for Pope Nicholas V. The message illustrated by the cycle of frescoes had to reflect the Pope's political-religious ideal of a Church founded on Apostolic authority while expressing the mission of charity and evangelizing. Accordingly, the Evangelists represented on the ceiling and the Fathers and Doctors of the Church on the arches emphasize the importance of the ecclesiastical tradition alongside the evangelical one. The choice of the two saints, Stephen and Lawrence, was intended instead to represent the mission of charity and proselytism. It is highly probably that Fra Angelico, although making use of assistants, was personally responsible for the concept and perhaps for the execution of the cycle as well, completed very rapidly. Although Benozzo Gozzoli was present beside Fra Angelico in the realization of the Niccolina frescoes, it is very difficult to determine where he may have been involved.

ism, transforming Rome into a workshop fervently occupied with translating and studying the classical texts. Nicholas V, a firm believer in the principle that figurative art could have a didactic function as well as the value of a refined political tool, commissioned Fra Angelico to fresco his small private chapel. The cycle, planned by the artist himself, was painted in a brief span of time thanks to the employment of assistants, among them the now expert Benozzo Gozzoli. It represents a precious document of the Pope's cultural interests as well as the narrative skill of the painter challenged by

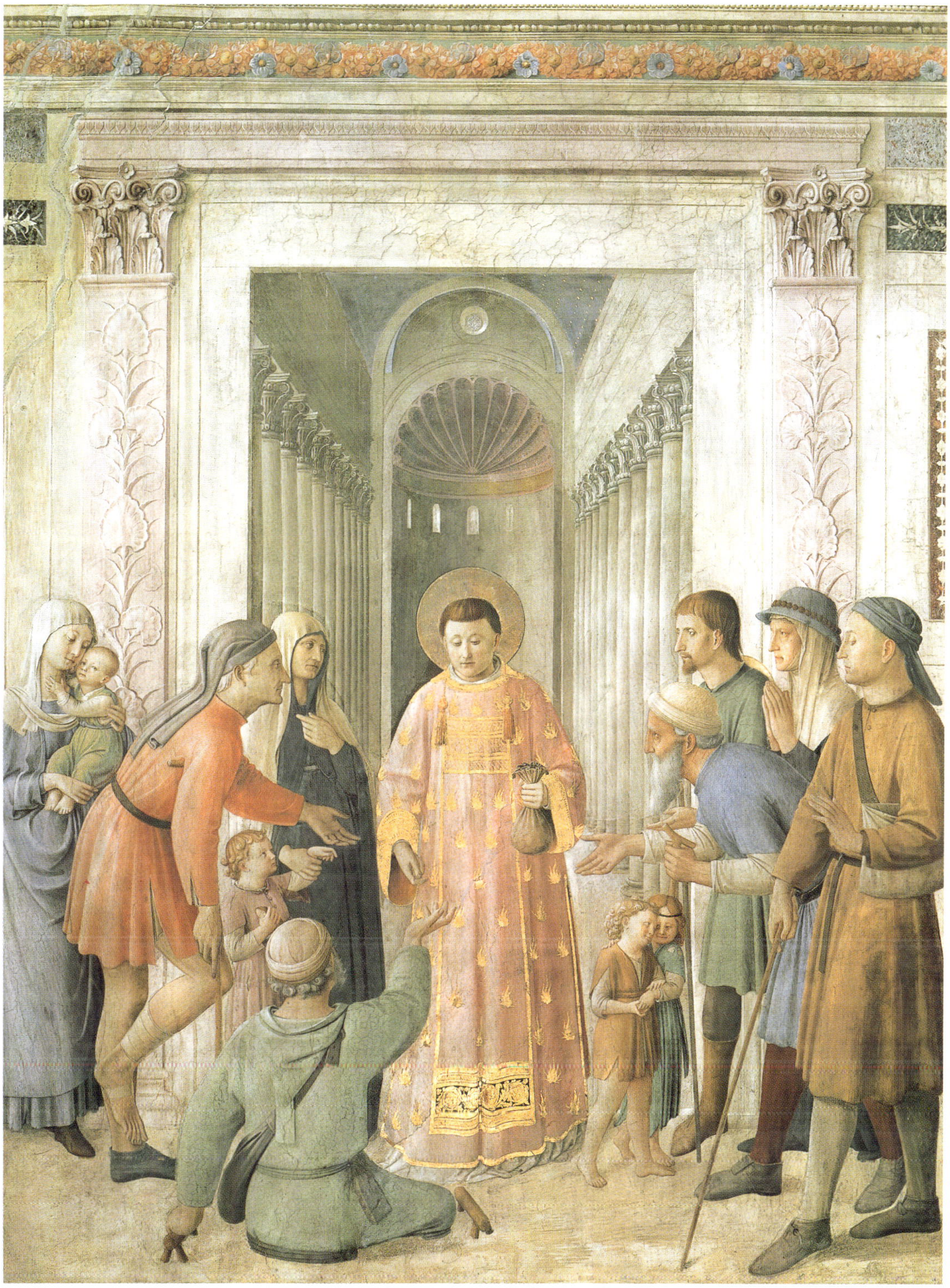

St Lawrence bestowing Alms, from the *Stories of St Lawrence*, 1448. Vatican City, Vatican Palaces, Niccolina Chapel.

One of the characteristics that make the Niccolina Chapel such an important document of 15th century painting is the consistent presence of architecture appearing in a wall decoration project. In fact, the scenes that illustrate the lives of Sts Stephen and Lawrence contain many accurate descriptions of urban architecture represented not only as illustration but also to create a realistic space within which the personages can move. In the episode shown here, as background to the figure of the saint appears a virtuosic line of receding arches, indicating the place of the scene. The close relationship between the saint and the basilica takes on a second meaning: the face of St Lawrence, perfectly positioned at the center of the Renaissance portal, marks the perspective focal point of the scene, while simultaneously indicating its symbolic centrality and identification with the Church itself.

the small room and its specific destination. In the lobes of the ceiling are the four figures of the Evangelists, while along the pilaster strips that divide the walls are portrayed eight Fathers and Doctors of the Church, two of them glories of the Eastern Church. These presences seem to underline the importance in the pictorial cycle of the tradition represented by the Evangelists, as well as the ecclesiastical tradition illustrated by the Doctors of the two Churches, Eastern and Western, according to the ecumenical ideal that had animated the recent Florentine Council.

On the walls, episodes from the lives of St Stephen and St Lawrence illustrate with narrative tones and classical elegance Pope's Humanist conception of the Church and of papal authority. The stories of St Stephen include *The Saint ordained Deacon* and *The bestowing of alms*, *The sermon*, *The dispute in the Synedrion*, *The expulsion* and *The martyrdom*. In similar manner, the stories of St Lawrence include *The Saint ordained Deacon*, *The Saint receiving the treasures of the Church from St Sixtus*, *The bestowing of alms*, *The Saint before the Prefect Decius* and *The martyrdom*. The choice of Stephen and Lawrence and the parallel narration of their lives was intended to suggest the idea of a Church that, attentive to the message of the Gospels, was active in the dual direction of charity and of preaching. Significant in the two stories is, in fact, the symmetrical repetition of the episodes of consecration, bestowing of alms on the poor and preaching or confessing the faith followed by martyrdom. Martyrdom represented the logical conclusion of the story, the culminating event which dramatically underscores the exemplary value of the saints' mandate. Perhaps the choice was also designed to celebrate the ideals and the virtues of the Pope himself, acknowledged to be gifted with extraordinary eloquence and uncommon generosity. Art historians have pointed out the originality of introducing into the language of the Niccolina Chapel numerous citations of the interiors and exteriors of historic buildings. To them is attributed the purpose of explicitly alluding to the Pope's project for urban renewal, to be carried out through large-scale initiatives for restoring and rearranging the ancient Roman monuments. Among the Pope's most ambitious plans was a vast project for rebuilding the original Basilica of St Peter's. The papal destination of the chapel, the subjects chosen and the need to convey a meaningful political and religious message must have urged Fra Angelico to adopt a pictorial language far from the intimate mysticism of the works in San Marco, suggesting to him a stately, noble style inspired by the atmosphere of Rome, abounding in classical memories, and by a didactic conception of history.

The date of Fra Angelico's return to Florence is unknown, but it took place in relation to a severe illness of his brother Benedetto, which was to prove fatal in 1450. Although his artistic production decreased after that date, Fra Angelico painted an altarpiece for the monastery of San Bonaventura at Bosco ai Frati, in the Mugello. The presence of Cosmas and Damian, protectors of the Medici, testifies that the work was commissioned by Cosimo the Elder who wished to donate it to the church which he had restored.

Among the artist's last works are the "istoriati" doors of the *Silverware Cupboard* for the oratory of the Santissima Annunziata, destined to contain the most precious of the votive offerings. The work was originally composed

Bosco ai Frati Altarpiece (Madonna and Child with Sts Anthony of Padova, Ludwig of Toulouse, Francis, Cosmas, Damian and Peter the Martyr), 1450-1452. Florence, San Marco Museum.

One of Fra Angelico's most refined works, the *Bosco ai Frati Altarpiece* shows the characteristic solemn, noble style of the Vatican frescoes. The architectural setting that serves as background to the scene emphasizes this resemblance. The enclosing wall inspired by Roman examples is broken by half-columns and niches arranged to frame the figures of the saints gathered around the Virgin. Within a shell-shaped vault simulating the apse of a basilica, she stands out against a splendid drapery of gilded fabric in which the brocade pattern can be distinguished. For the aulic setting and the precious effects of the marbleized floor decoration and golden fabric, the altarpiece seems to present features designed to appeal to the taste of such a wealthy, prominent client as Cosimo the Elder.

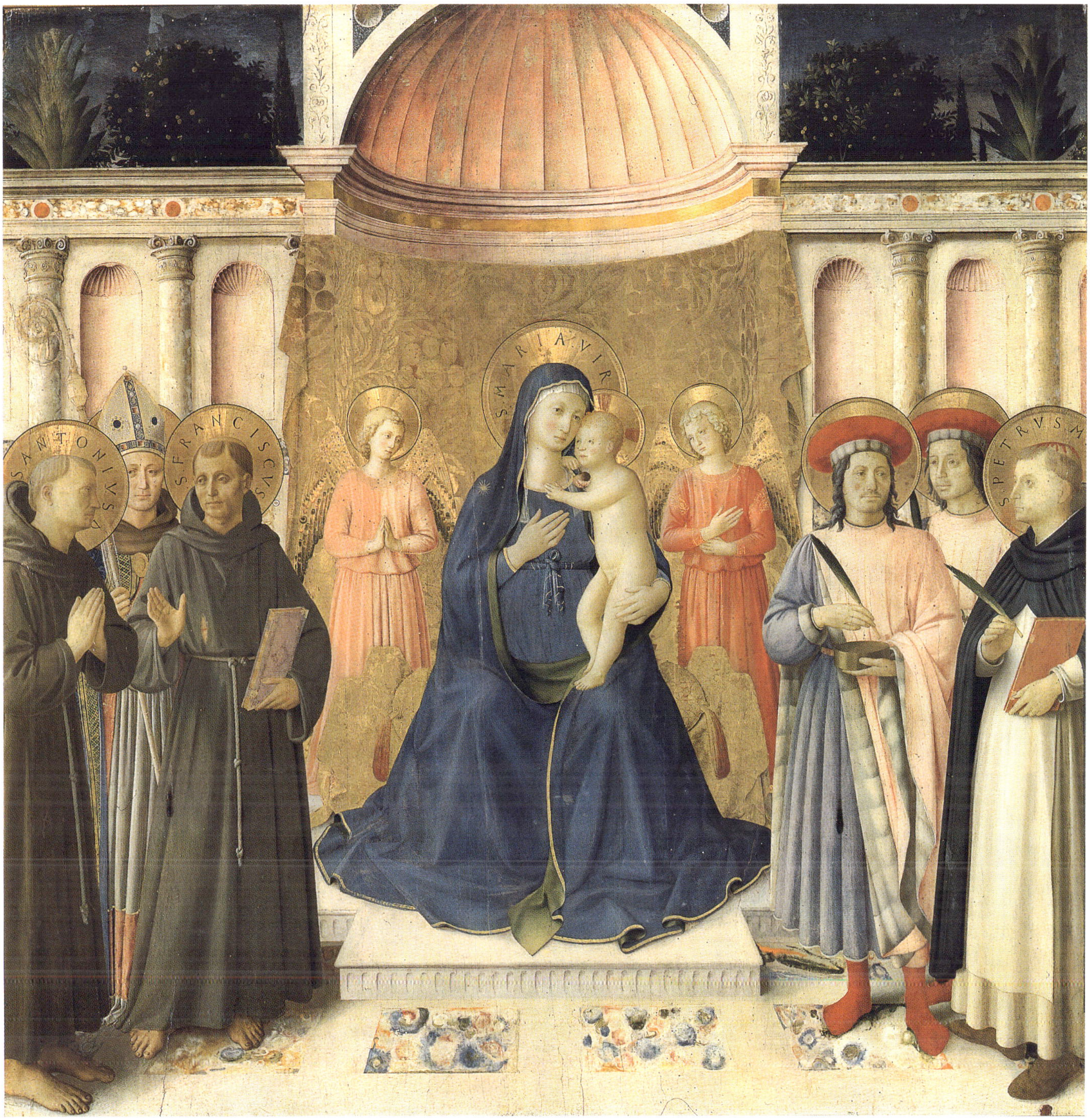

of forty panels by Fra Angelico and his assistants, thirty-two of which are now in the San Marco Museum. The important client was Piero de' Medici, son of Cosimo the Elder. The *Silverware Cupboard* seems to be the last work left us by the artist who, around 1453, made a last mysterious journey to Rome, perhaps to paint the altarpiece destined to adorn the high altar of the church of Santa Maria sopra Minerva, whose restoration was completed during that year. In 1455 Fra Angelico died and on his tomb, in the chapel of St Thomas Aquinas, in the same church, two epitaphs which may have been written by Pope Nicholas V celebrated in aulic tones that "angelic" painter, the erudite and devout messenger of religious Humanism.

Silverware Cupboard, whole and detail of the panel portraying the *Vision of Ezekiel* (shown here), c. 1450-1452. Florence, San Marco Museum.

Originally the *Silverware Cupboard* was formed of a group of panels (some now lost) destined to cover the cabinet containing the most precious church furnishings of Santissima Annunziata. They must have been inserted in a mechanism that rose and descended driven by a pulley. The group contains evangelical scenes, from the Annunciation to the Pentecost, preceded by the *Mystic Wheel*. At the lower corners of this scene are Ezekiel, ecstatic in his vision, and Gregory the Great, fragments of whose works appear in inscriptions in the upper corners of the panel. Two concentric circles contain the figures of the Evangelists and the authors of the Epistles (inside) and twelve prophets (outside). The role of Fra Angelico in this work appears limited to the concept of the complex iconographic program, while ample space seems to have been left to his assistants.

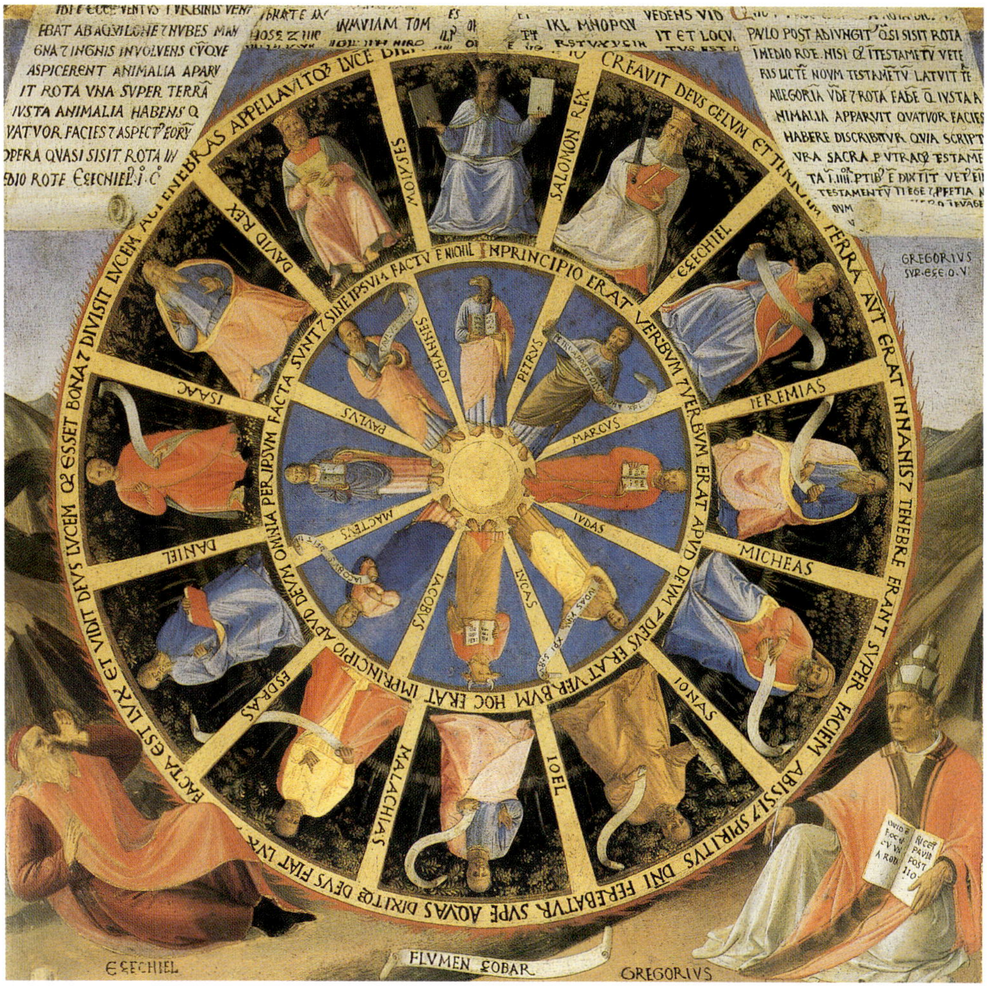

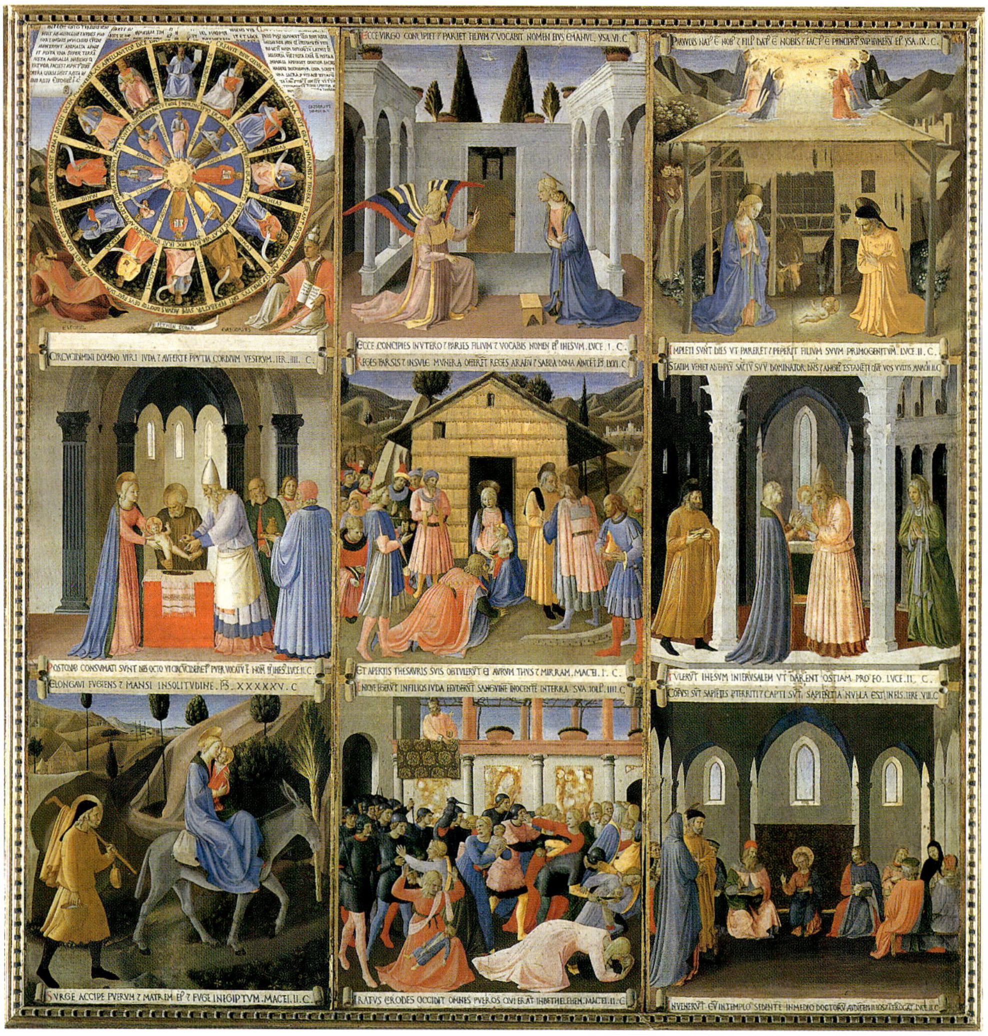

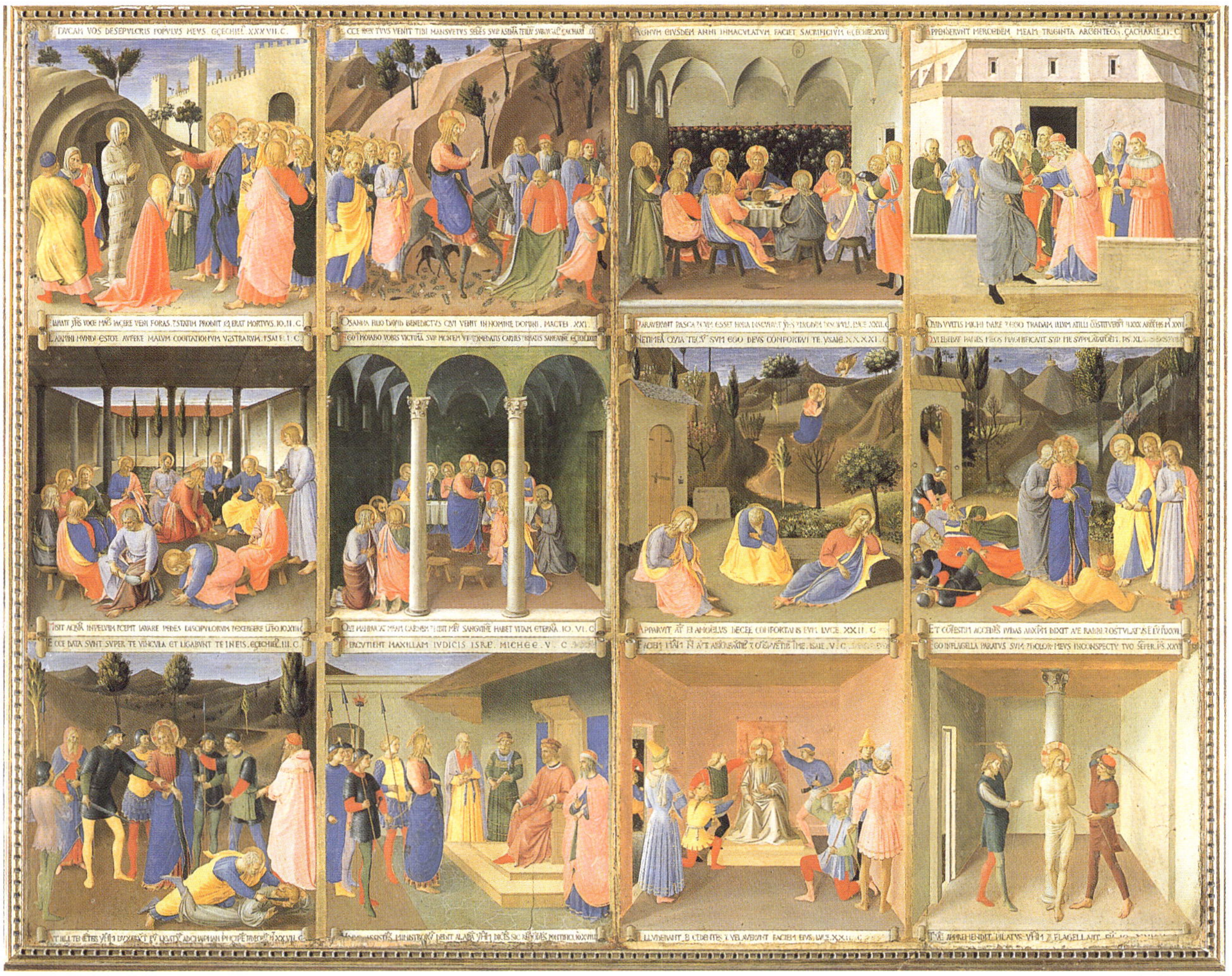

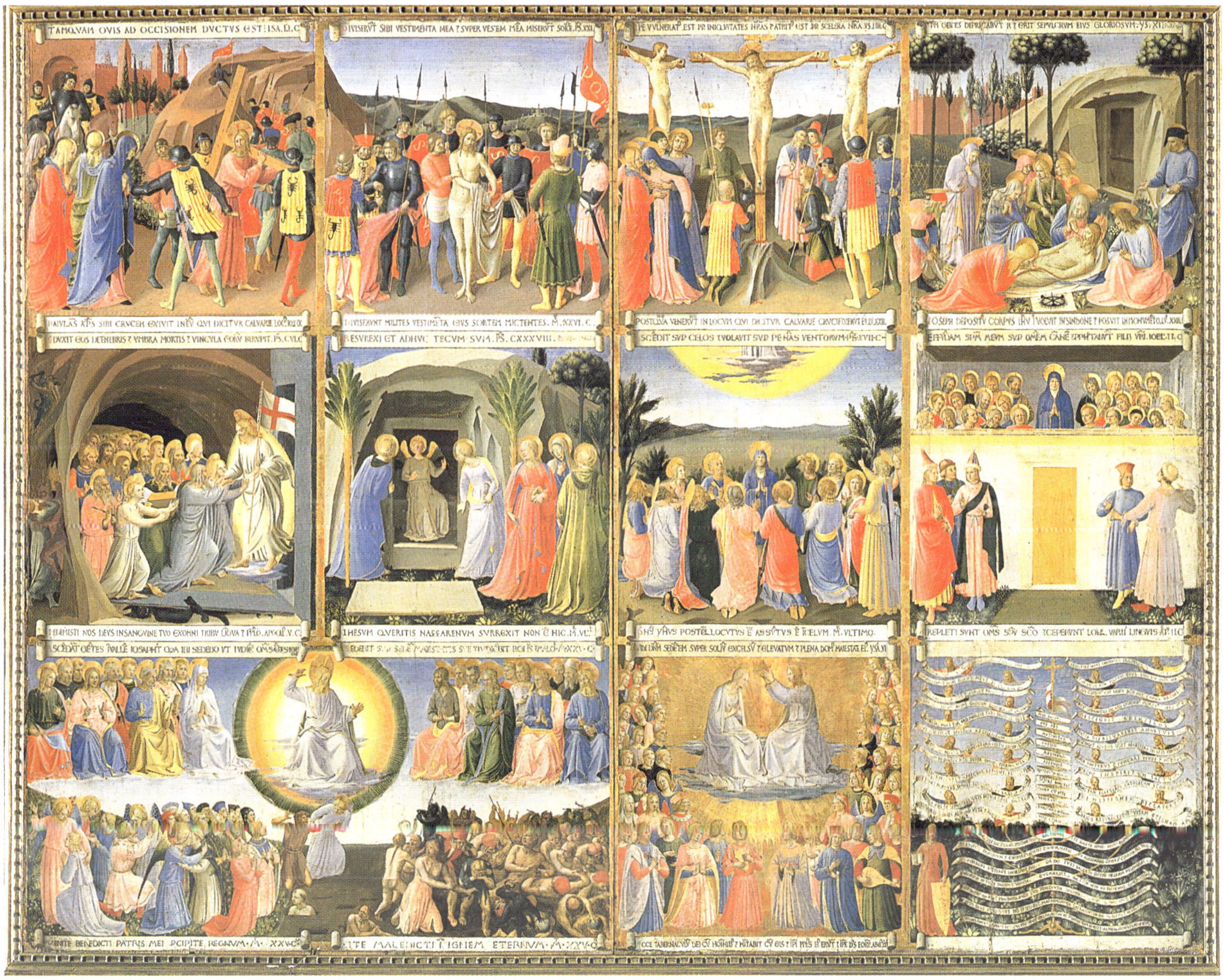

Chronology	1385	1415	1420	1425	1430
Fra Angelico	**1385** Sometime between this year and 1400 Guido di Piero is born near Vicchio in the Mugello. His younger brother, Benedetto, is to follow him in the ecclesiastical career, his sister Checca is to have a son, Giovanni di Antonio, who will assist the painter in the worksites of Rome and Orvieto.	**1417** Guido di Piero, a layman already called "dipintore", becomes a member of the Compagnia di San Niccolò del Carmine. **1418** A document records payment to Fra Angelico for a panel painted for the Florentine church of Santo Stefano al Ponte.	**1420-1422** In these years Fra Angelico joins a religious order, entering the Dominican monastery at Fiesole in 1421. Here he is to leave important decorations as well as the *San Domenico Altarpiece*. **1423** In the payment for a *Crucifix* for Santa Maria Nuova he is mentioned as Fra Giovanni.	**1429** The monastery of San Pietro Martire is recorded as owing money to that of Fiesole for an altarpiece by Fra Angelico. In this same year Palla Strozzi commissions him to complete the *Santa Trinita Altarpiece*, left unfinished in 1425 by Lorenzo Monaco, which is put in place three years later.	**1432** The Servite Brothers of Brescia commission a now lost *Annunciation* of Fra Angelico, who is appointed vicar of the Fiesole monastery. **1433** The Linen-drapers' Guild commissions of him a tabernacle for the church of Orsanmichele, whose wooden frame had been designed by Ghiberti.
Florence	**1385-1387** *Stories of the True Cross* by Agnolo Gaddi in Santa Croce. **1398** *Treatise on painting* by Cennino Cennini. **1401** The Arte di Calimala announces a competition for the second door of the Baptistery. At San Giovanni Valdarno, Masaccio is born. **1412** *The four crowned saints* by Nanni di Banco.	**1417** Masaccio comes to Florence from Valdarno, Lorenzo Monaco emerges among the Florentine painters. Donatello sculpts the *St George* for Orsanmichele. **1418** Brunelleschi wins the competition for the Cathedral dome. **1419** Spedale degli Innocenti, designed by Brunelleschi.	**1422** Brunelleschi designs the Old Sacristy for the Basilica of San Lorenzo, rebuilt in 1419. **1423** *Adoration of the Magi* by Gentile da Fabriano for the Strozzi Chapel in Santa Trinita. **1424** Masolino and Masaccio fresco the Brancacci Chapel.	**1425** Gentile paints the *Quaratesi Polyptych*, influenced by Florentine innovation. **1426** Masaccio paints the *Pisa Polyptych*, today divided among several museums. **1427** Tomb of the anti-pope John XXIII by Donatello and Michelozzo in the Florence Baptistery.	**1433** Donatello and Luca della Robbia sculpt the *Cantorie* for the Duomo. Cosimo the Elder is exiled; the next year, when he returns to the city, the political rise to power of the Medici and their allies begins.
Rome	**1402-1404** Donatello and Brunelleschi are in Rome to study ancient art. **1410** Pope Alexander V begins the work of enlarging the Vatican Palaces.	**1417** Oddone Colonna becomes Pope under the name of Martin V. In 1419 he meets Gentile da Fabriano at Brescia and invites him to Rome in view of his plan for the city's artistic rebirth.	**1420** Martin V makes his entry into Rome after the papacy's long absence from the city. Piero della Francesca is born at Città di Castello. **1422** Arcangelo di Cola, follower of Gentile da Fabriano, is in Rome at the service of the Pope. **1423** Martin V proclaims the Jubilee.	**1427** Gentile da Fabriano is in Rome with Pisanello; at his master's death, he inherits his shop and remains in the city until 1433. **1428** Masaccio and Masolino paint the *Triptych of the Snow*; during this work Masaccio dies.	**1431** Eugene IV is elected Pope. Masolino finishes the frescoes in San Clemente at Rome. **1432-1433** Donatello's second stay in Rome. **1434** The *Descriptio urbis Romae* by Alberti is the first systematic description of the ancient city's monuments.
Milan, Venice and Bologna	**1386** The workshop for the Milan cathedral is opened, at the initiative of Gian Galeazzo Visconti; a few years later work begins on San Petronio in Bologna. Dating from the end of the century is the *Notebook of drawings* by Giovannino de' Grassi, architect of the Duomo.	**1415** In Venice, Gentile da Fabriano and Pisanello work on the cycle of frescoes with stories of Federico Barbarossa for the Sala del Maggior Consiglio in Palazzo Ducale, now lost.	**1420** *Mystic marriage of St Catherine* by Michelino da Besozzo. *Madonna of the Rose Bush* by Stefano da Verona reveals the influence of the courtly Gothic style from France. **1421** Work begins on the Ca' d'Oro of Venice, masterpiece of late Gothic architecture.	**1425** Paolo Uccello is in Venice, where he executes a lost mosaic for the Basilica of San Marco; he will remain there until 1430. **1427** The work of enlarging Palazzo Ducale is completed.	**1430-1431** Giovanni Bellini and Carlo Crivelli are born in Venice, Andrea Mantegna in Padova, Vincenzo Foppa in Brescia, Cosmè Tura in Ferrara. **1433** Peace of Ferrara between Milan and Florence. Cosimo de' Medici, in exile at Padova along with his architect Michelozzo, disseminates the new Florentine art.
Naples and Palermo	**1386** Carlo III Durazzo is succeeded by his son Ladislao, who reigns over Naples until 1414. Near the end of the century the Gothic-Calatalonian and Franco-Burgandian school spreads in Sicily.	**1415** In the first half of the century many artists work in Sicily, among them the Pisan painter Turino Vanni, Pisanello and perhaps the Turin Jaquerio.	**1420** Pope Martin V and the Sforza family join forces to restore the Angevins to the throne of Naples. **1423** Alfonso d'Aragona fails in his attempt to annex Naples to Sicily. Queen Giovanna adopts Louis III d'Angiò.	**1427** Donatello and Michelozzo, who had opened a workshop in 1425, build the tomb of Cardinal Rinaldo Brancaccio in Naples, at Sant'Angelo a Nilo.	**1430** Antonello da Messina is born. Around the middle of the century he trains in Naples, where the influence of Flemish painting is strong.

1435	1440	1445	1450	1455	1460
1438 Possibly the year when the Cortona *Annunciation* and the *Perugia Polyptych* were painted. Michelozzo begins work on reconstructing the Florentine monastery of San Marco, which Fra Angelico and his assistants fresco starting in the following year. The cycle is completed in 1446.	**1442** The work in San Marco continues: by August the Chapter House with the *Crucifixion* is certainly completed. **1443** On January 6, the day of the Epiphany, the church of San Marco is reconsecrated by Pope Eugene IV. Fra Angelico is procurator of the monastery.	**1445-1446** Eugene IV calls him to work on the apse of St Peter's and the Apostolic Palace. **1447** He frescoes the ceiling of the Chapel of San Brizio in the Orvieto Duomo (with Benozzo). **1448** He returns to Rome to decorate the studiolo of Nicholas V (destroyed) and the Niccolina Chapel.	**1450** Prior of the Fiesole monastery, he paints the *Head of Christ* and the *Bosco ai Frati Altarpiece.* **1452** The *Silverware Cabinet* is finished. **1453** Last and definitive stay in Rome of Fra Angelico, summoned perhaps by Cardinal Torquemada to work in Santa Maria sopra Minerva.	**1455** On February 18 he dies in Rome, is buried in the Chapel of St Thomas in Santa Maria sopra Minerva.	**1469** Domenico di Giovanni da Corella calls him "angelicus pictor". **1481** "Angelical and devout and affected and highly ornate, done with great ease" (Landino). **1568** Vasari codifies the image of the painter-monk: "Truly angelical father, worthy priest, gentle and devout". Proclaimed blessed in 1982 .
1435 Alberti writes his *De pictura*. Donatello sculpts the *Annunciation* for Santa Croce. **1436** Brunelleschi's dome is inaugurated. Paolo Uccello: *Monument to Giovanni Acuto*. **1439** Ecumenical council. Domenico Veneziano and Piero della Francesca work in Sant'Egidio.	**1441** Filippo Lippi is commissioned to paint the *Coronation of the Virgin* altarpiece (Uffizi) for the church of Sant'Ambrogio. **1444** Michelozzo designs for Cosimo the Elder Palazzo Medici-Riccardi, prototype of the lordly Renaissance mansion.	**1445** Botticelli is born. **1446** Work begins on Palazzo Rucellai designed by Alberti. Paolo Uccello frescoes the Green Cloister in Santa Maria Novella. **1447** Andrea del Castagno paints *The Last Supper* in Sant'Apollonia. **1449** Lorenzo the Magnificent is born.	**1451** Cycle of *Famous men* by Andrea del Castagno for the Villa Medici di Legnaia. **1452** Piero della Francesca frescoes the *Stories of the True Cross* in San Francesco at Arezzo, finished in 1466. Filippo Lippi decorates the High Chapel in the Prato Duomo. Leonardo da Vinci is born.	**1456** Alberti designs the facade of Santa Maria Novella for Giovanni Rucellai. Around this date Paolo Uccello paints the three versions of the *Battle of San Romano.* **1457** Filippino Lippi, son of Filippo, is born. **1459** Benozzo Gozzoli frescoes the Chapel of the Magi in Palazzo Medici.	**1463** Marsilio Ficino founds the Platonic Academy of Careggi. **1475** At Caprese, near Arezzo, Michelangelo is born. **1482-1485** It is presumed that Botticelli's *Primavera* and *The Birth of Venus* date from these years.
1435 Filarete is in Rome; since 1433 he has worked on the bronze door for the Basilica of St Peter's, manifesto of Roman Humanism.	**1444** Journey of the Frenchman Jean Fouquet to Italy; in Rome, where he paints a now lost portrait of Pope Eugene IV, he meets Fra Angelico.	**1447** At the death of Eugene IV, the papal throne passes to Nicholas V, who begins work on the Vatican Palaces. Cosimo de' Medici assumes the role of banker and financer of the Church's initiatives. **1448** Lorenzo Valla is called to Rome as Apostolic Secretary.	**1452** Nicholas V commissions Bernardo Rossellino to enlarge St Peter's Basilica with a new apse. Alberti dedicates his *De re aedificatoria* to the Pope. **1453** Starting from this date Fra Angelico and Benozzo Gozzoli are engaged in the Roman worksites.	**1455** Nicholas V dies: Giannozzo Manetti writes a biography of the Humanist Pope. Succeeded by Callisto III (the Spaniard Alfonso Borgia).	**1465** Pomponio Leto founds the Accademia Romana, disbanded three years later by Pope Paul II for suspected impiety. **1480** The Domus Aurea is discovered. **1481-1482** Botticelli and Perugino fresco the Sistine Chapel. **1483** Raphael is born in Urbino.
1435 Cardinal Branda Castiglione summons Masolino to fresco the Baptistery and the Collegiate of Castiglione Olona (Varese). **1438** Pisanello paints the *Vision of St Eustachius* and perhaps begins the frescoes in Sant'Anastasia at Verona.	**1442** Andrea del Castagno is in Venice. **1443** Donatello goes to Padova, remains until 1453, leaving works such as the monument to the Gattamelata and the Altar of the Saint. **1445** Jacopo Bellini paints the Louvre *Virgin and Child.*	**1448** Mantegna frescoes the Ovetari Chapel at Padova. **1449** Lo Squarcione, whose shop represents a forging place for many Veneto artists, paints around this date the polyptych with St Jerome.	**1450** Alberti begins the Tempio Malatestiano at Rimini, which Piero della Francesca will decorate with the fresco of *Sigismondo Malatesta* the next year. Ercole de' Roberti is born in Ferrara.	**1455** Peace of Lodi among Milan, Venice, Florence and Naples. **1456** Filarete designs the Ospedale Maggiore in Milan for Francesco Sforza.	**1477-1478** Giorgione is born at Castelfranco Veneto. Around 1480 Titian is born at Pieve di Cadore. **1498** Leonardo frescoes the *Last Supper* at Santa Maria delle Grazie in Milan.
1435 Queen Giovanna dies and the Aragons again make claims to the throne. The Humanist Lorenzo Valla is in Naples, during his stay he publishes the text that unveils the historical falsehood of the donation of Constantine (1440).	**1440** Colantonio's workshop, open to French and Spanish influences, is active in Naples. **1442** Alfonso d'Aragona manages to conquer the Kingdom of Naples, overthrowing Renato d'Angiò. **1444** Colantonio paints the polyptych for San Lorenzo Maggiore.	**1445** Contacts with the Flemish are intensified: a painting by Van Eyck arrives at Naples for Alfonso d'Aragona, Jean Fouquet is in the city. **1446** Dating from this year is the imposing fresco the *Triumph of Death* in Palazzo Sclafani at Palermo (now in the National Gallery).	**1453** In Naples work is intensified on the Arch commemorating Alfonso d'Aragona, a Renaissance interpretation of the Roman arch of triumph, in whose realization collaborate Pietro da Milano, Francesco Laurana and Mino da Fiesole.	**1456** Bartolomeo Facio's *De viris illustribus* celebrates the artists most esteemed by the Neapolitan court: Gentile da Fabriano, Pisanello, Ghiberti, Donatello, as well as the Flemish Van Eyck and Van der Weyden.	**1471-1474** Antonello da Messina paints *Our Lady of the Annunciation* and *St Jerome in his Study*.

CORONATION OF THE VIRGIN

Among the masterpieces by Fra Angelico dating from the decade of the 1430s, the altarpiece was painted, like the Madrid *Annunciation*, for an altar in San Domenico at Fiesole, where it was still to be seen at the time of Vasari. The heavenly court is depicted in sumptuous tones and glowing colors, made even more vivid by the golden light enveloping the entire scene. At the top of a majestic stairway, whose marbleized decoration is exquisitely rendered, the act of coronation takes place under a gilded late Gothic baldachin. The work is embellished by ornamental details described with extraordinary care and analytic sprit. Decorative accents appear in the embroidered mantles of the onlookers, in the copes, crosiers, miters, precious book bindings, jewel-studded crowns and the fine details of the fabrics. A bishop saint in the foreground, seen from the back, holds up a cope embroidered with easily readable stories from the life of Christ. The skilful perspective scheme guides the viewer's eye to the culmination of the scene through two levels: the chiaroscuro of the flooring produced by numerous rows of majolica tiles and the multicolored stairway with its marbleized steps. This complex expedient demonstrates the artist's knowledge of scientific perspective, and also reveals a personal and highly virtuosic elaboration of the lesson taught by Masaccio. It has been suggested that the panel is to be identified with a *Coronation* mentioned in the *Chronicles* of the Fiesole monastery along with another of Fra Angelico's works, the *San Domenico Altarpiece*. On the predella unfolds a sequence of episodes from the life of St Dominic: *The dream of Innocent III* (shown here), *The apparition of Sts Peter and Paul to St Dominic*, *The healing of Napoleone Orsini*, *Christ dead*, *The dispute of St Dominic and the miracle of the book*, *The angels serving supper to the monks* and *The death of St Dominic*.

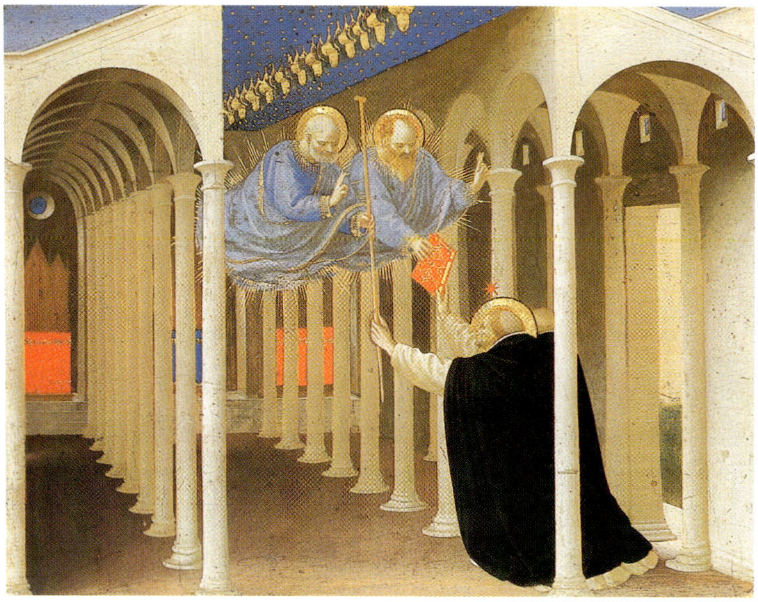

Coronation of the Virgin
tempera and gold on wood
213 x 211 (main panel), 29.5 x 210 (predella); c. 1430
Paris, The Louvre

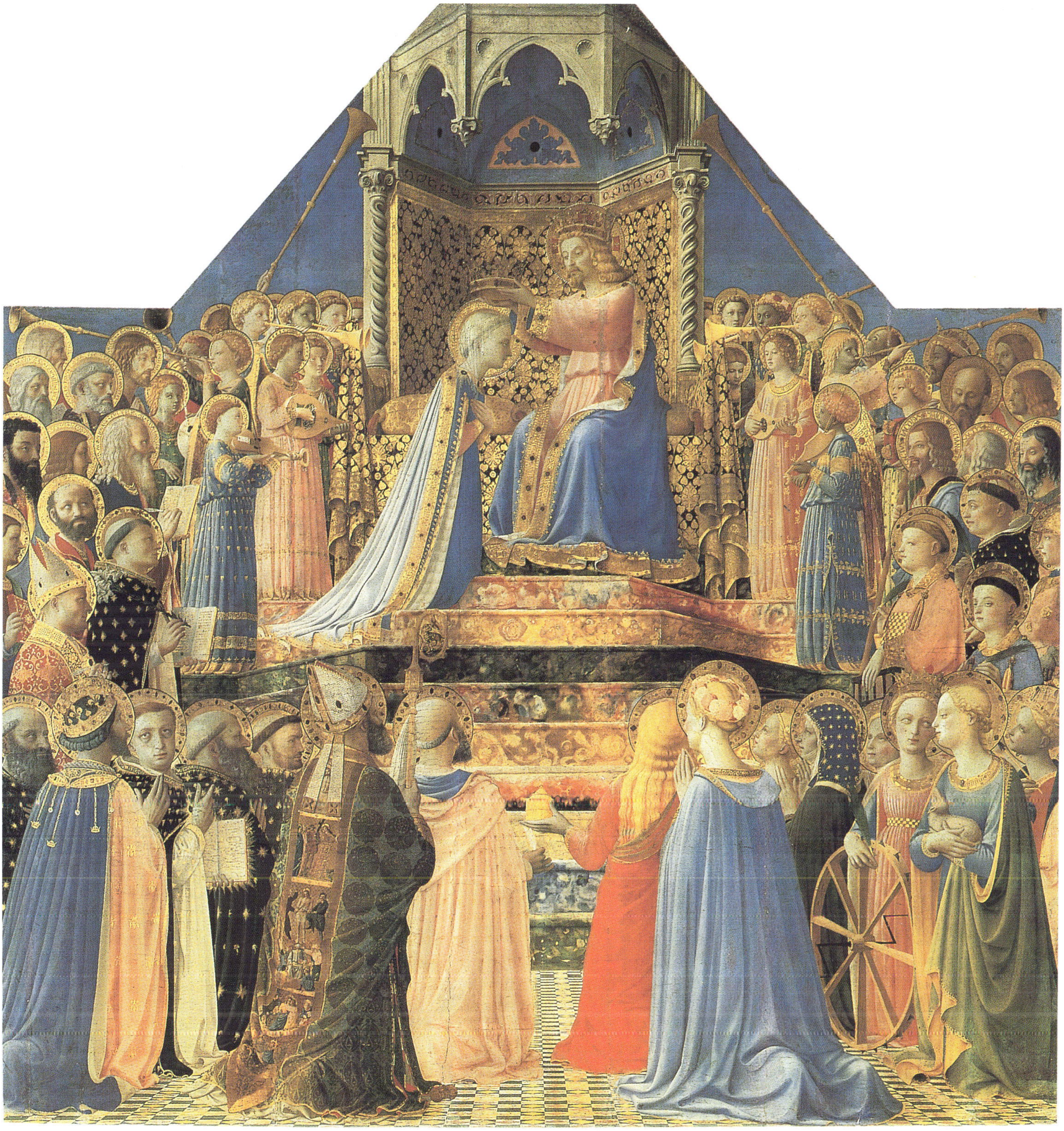

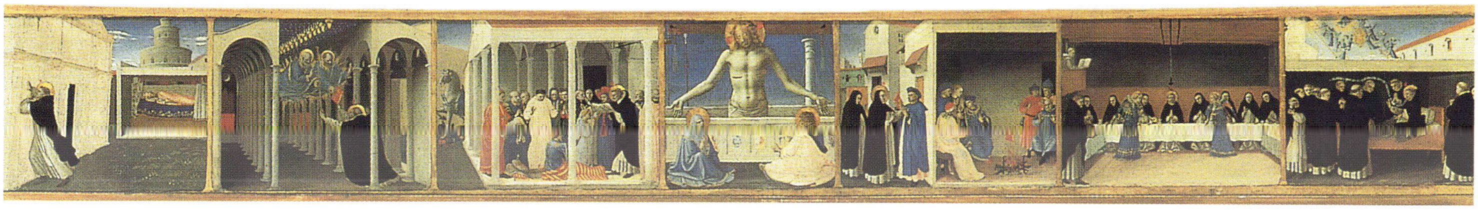

DEPOSITION
(SANTA TRINITA ALTARPIECE)

Commissioned of Lorenzo Monaco, who had painted the cusps and the predella, this altarpiece had remained unfinished at the painter's death in 1425. The decision of Palla Strozzi, renowned for his humanistic interests, to entrust the work to Fra Angelico seems to emphasis their affinity of intentions. A document from 1432 records a payment made to a carpenter for installing the painting in Santa Trinita; by that date then, the *Deposition* had already been finished. The division into three parts of the work, barely indicated by the flowery wooden arches in late Gothic style, is reiterated in the triple grouping of the inscriptions in classical characters at the foot of the altarpiece, erudite citations of Fra Angelico the theologian and homage paid to the patron's philological interests. A similar explanation seems applicable to the inscriptions on the gilded haloes and the small panel at the top of the cross with their mixed Greek, Latin and Hebrew characters, a reference to Florentine humanist circles. Among the onlookers and the leading figures are personages in modern dress whose faces show the strongly delineated features typical of portraits. Palla Strozzi and his son Lorenzo have been recognized in the man holding up the instruments of the Passion and in the young kneeling Blessed One. The fact that a reliquary of the True Cross was kept in Santa Trinita confers on the crown of thorns and the nails an intense, specific link between the work and the church in which it was placed. According to Vasari, the face of Nicodemus was that of the great architect Michelozzo, today commonly thought to be instead the personage wearing the black hat. The painting reveals a broad range of aspects, from introspective capacity in portraying faces and emotions to realism in the rendering of vegetation and the landscape, from perspective skill in representing real space and conferring three-dimensional volume on the human figures to mysticism in the finely modulated use of light and the chromatic research of the enameled colors. The contemporary presence of Lorenzo Monaco and that of Fra Angelico makes this work an interesting document of transition from the late Gothic style to one that is fully Renaissance in expression. In the cusps are the scenes of *Noli me tangere*, of the *Ascension* and of the *Maries at the tomb*, while the slender pilasters on the front and sides of the painting bear images of saints, among them the splendid figure of *St Michael Archangel*.

***Deposition* (*Santa Trinita Altarpiece*)**
tempera and gold on wood
185 x 176; 1431-1432
Florence, San Marco Museum

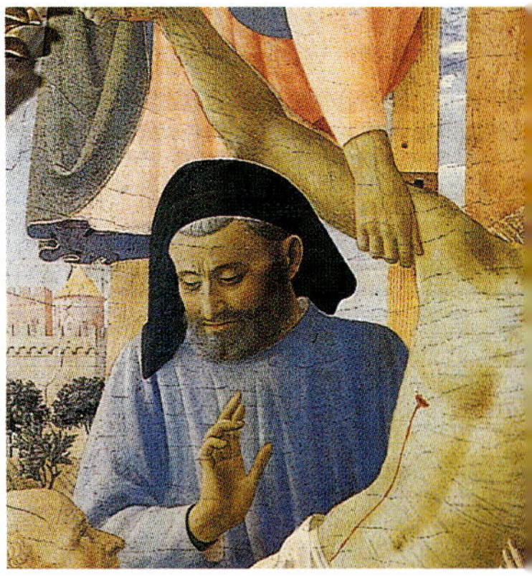

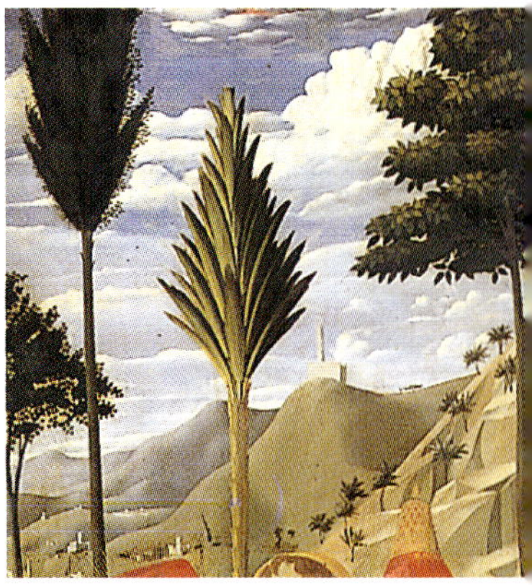

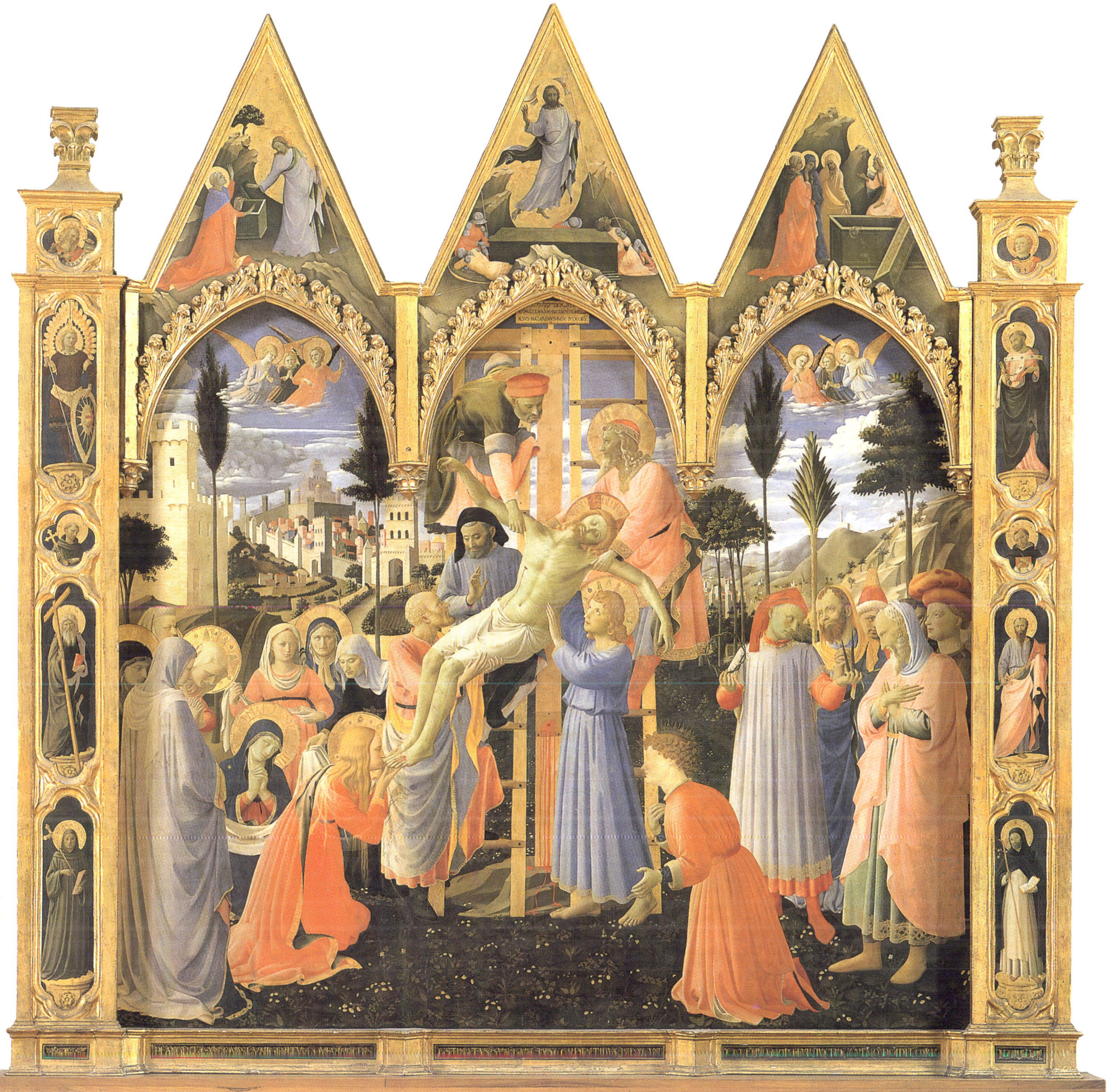

TABERNACLE OF THE LINEN DRAPERS

For this work the Linaiuoli, or Linen Drapers' Guild, had established a very substantial recompense, which seems to confirm the leading role held by Fra Angelico in the Florence of the 15th century's fourth decade. The year before this same Guild had commissioned Lorenzo Ghiberti to design the wooden structure of the Tabernacle, whose profile with triangular tympanum and serrated band recalls the architecture of the niche in Orsanmichele which housed this same sculptor's *St Matthew*. Painted both inside and out, as requested by the client, the Tabernacle presents at the center of the aedicule a statuary Madonna wearing her characteristic blue mantle, skillfully draped. Standing on his mother's knees, a solemn Christ Child bestowing blessings bears in his left hand a golden globe, symbol of regality. Within this space, covered by a starry vault, forcefully emerges the image of the Holy Ghost. The drapery of the Virgin's mantle and the precious damasked fabric covering her chair as well as the gilded curtain opened to show the scene represent a sort of homage to the activity of the patron Guild, a corporation whose members were the city's producers and merchants of fabrics. The four figures of saints painted on both sides of the doors, inspired perhaps by the sculptures of Ghiberti, appear monumental. They are St John the Baptist and St Mark on the inner sides, and St Mark, portrayed twice insofar as patron saint of the Guild, and St Peter on the outer sides. In the richly draped mantles, obviously classical in style, can be glimpsed the lesson of Ghiberti's humanism, strongly inspired by ancient sculpture and clearly expressed in the reliefs on the third door of the Baptistery of St John. The possible influence of Ghiberti on Fra Angelico seems to emerge also in the musical angels on the frame, very similar to the figures adorning the frame of the Baptistery's third door. In the predella, which depicts the episodes of *St Peter preaching in the presence of St Mark*, the *Adoration of the Magi* and the *Martyrdom of St Mark*, the style appears changed and the decoration becomes rich in architectural details, among which it seems possible to recognize Palazzo Vecchio.

Tabernacle of the Linen Drapers (Madonna with Child and Sts Mark, Peter, John the Baptist and Mark)
tempera and gold on wood
250 x 133 (closed doors), 250 x 266 (open doors);
1433-1435
Florence, San Marco Museum

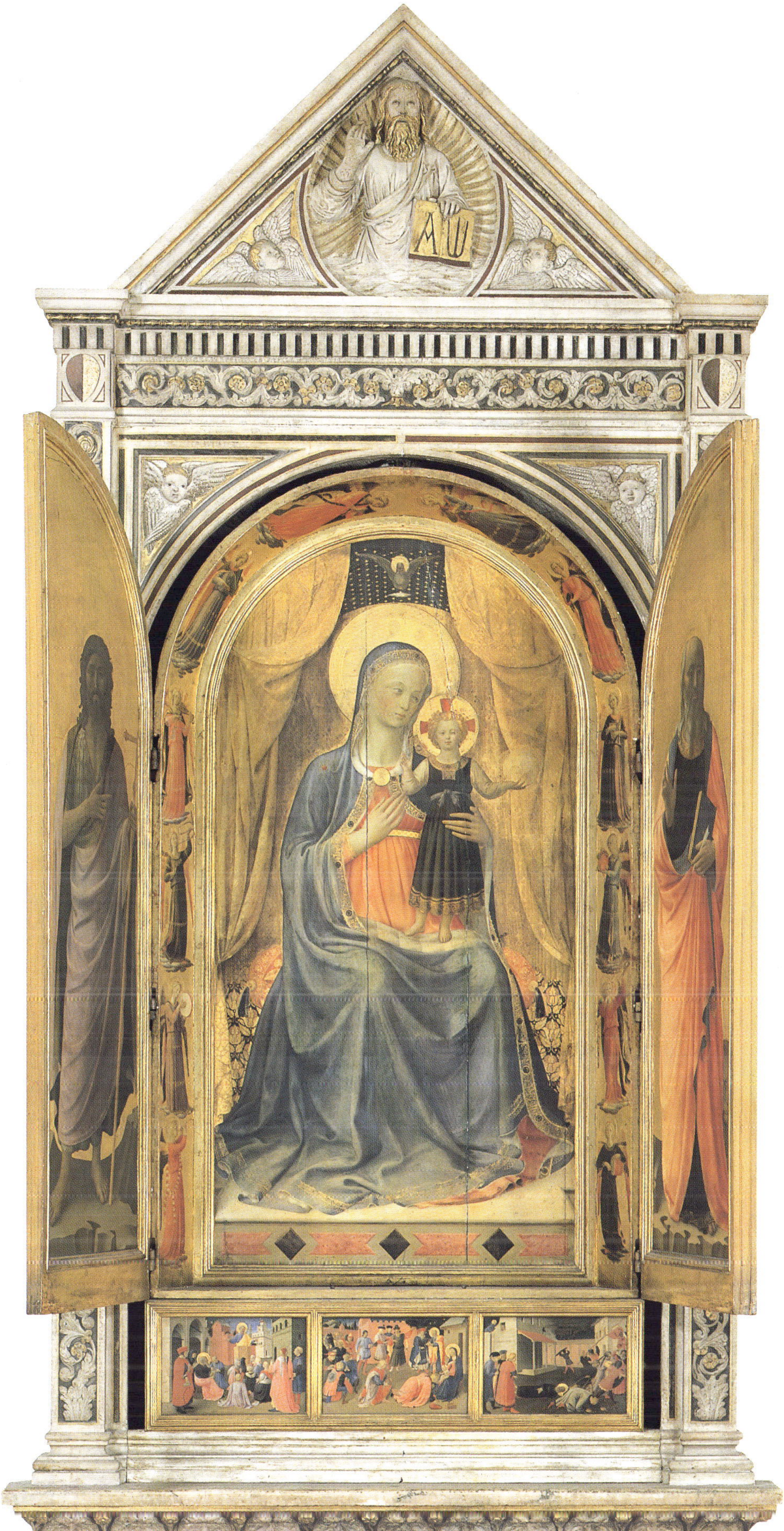

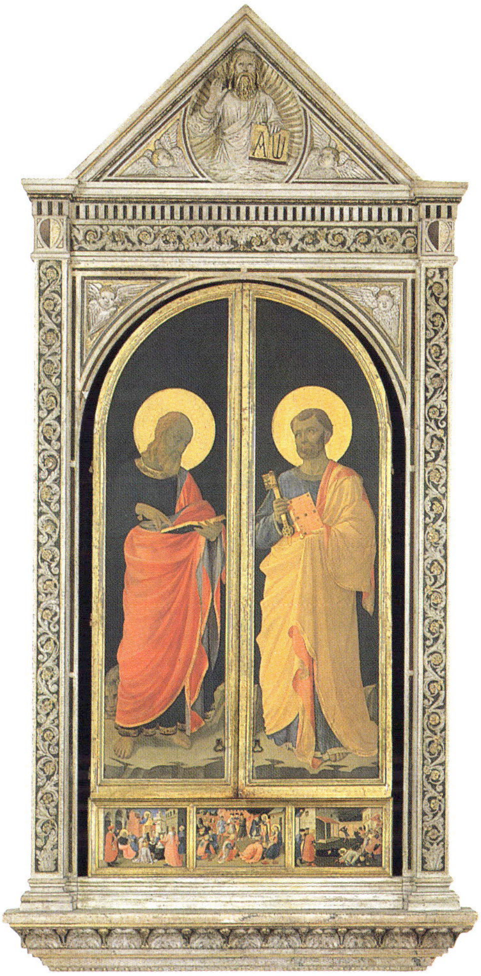

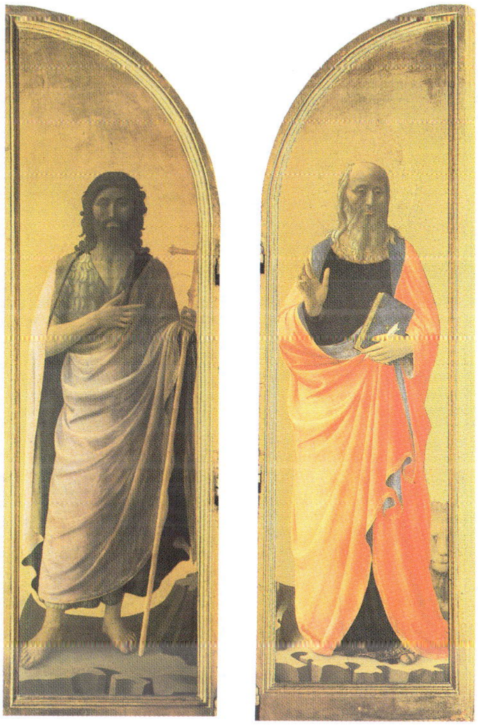

ANNALENA ALTARPIECE

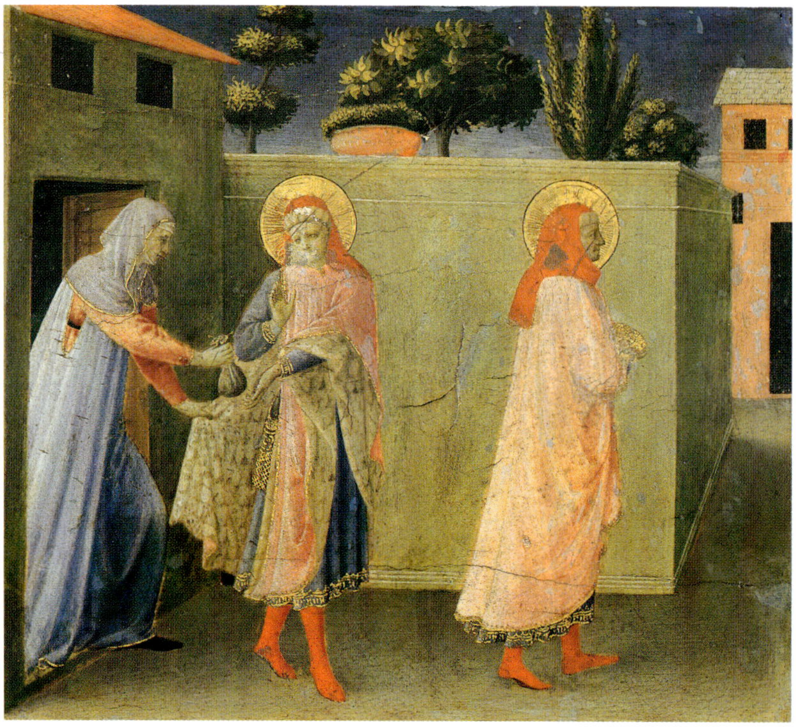

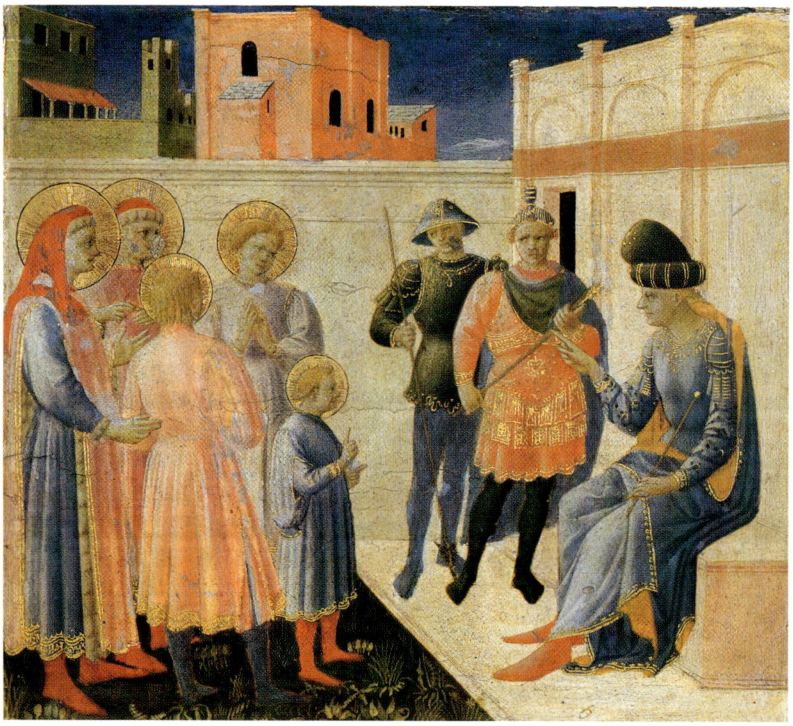

This work shows a turning away from the old polyptych structure in favor of a decidedly unitary composition. Dating from around the middle of the fourth decade of the 15th century, the painting, whose original location is unknown, takes the name of the convent of San Vincenzo di Annalena.

Appearing in the work, with clearly classical tones, are Sts Cosmas and Damian, patron saints of physicians ("medici" in Italian) and by extension of the Medici family.

The presence of St Lawrence has also suggested that the painting may have come from the Medici chapel in the church dedicated to this saint, and may therefore be dated at 1434, the year in which Cosimo the Elder returned to the city after his brief period of exile.

Dating from this same year is a document in which Brunelleschi stated that in the Basilica of St Lawrence should be placed only panels of square shape and without ornaments, that is, without cusps or partitions of late Gothic style, more in harmony with his exquisitely Renaissance architecture.

With the modernized forms of the *Annalena Altarpiece* Fra Angelico showed his ability to comply with the elegant innovations of Brunelleschi's architecture. In minutely detailed narrative language the predella relates the stories of the Saints Cosmas and Damian: *The healing of Palladia*, *The Saints before Lysia*, *The Saints saved from drowning*, *The Saints condemned to the stake in vain* (shown here), *The Saints crucified and stoned in vain*, *The martyrdom of the Saints* (all now in the San Marco Museum) and *The healing of the Deacon Giustiniano* (in a private collection).

***The Annalena Altarpiece* (*Madonna with Child and the Sts Peter the Martyr, Damian, Cosmas, John the Evangelist, Lawrence and Francis*)**
tempera and gold on wood
180 x 202 (main panel), 20 x 22 (each section of the predella); 1434-1435
Florence, San Marco Museum

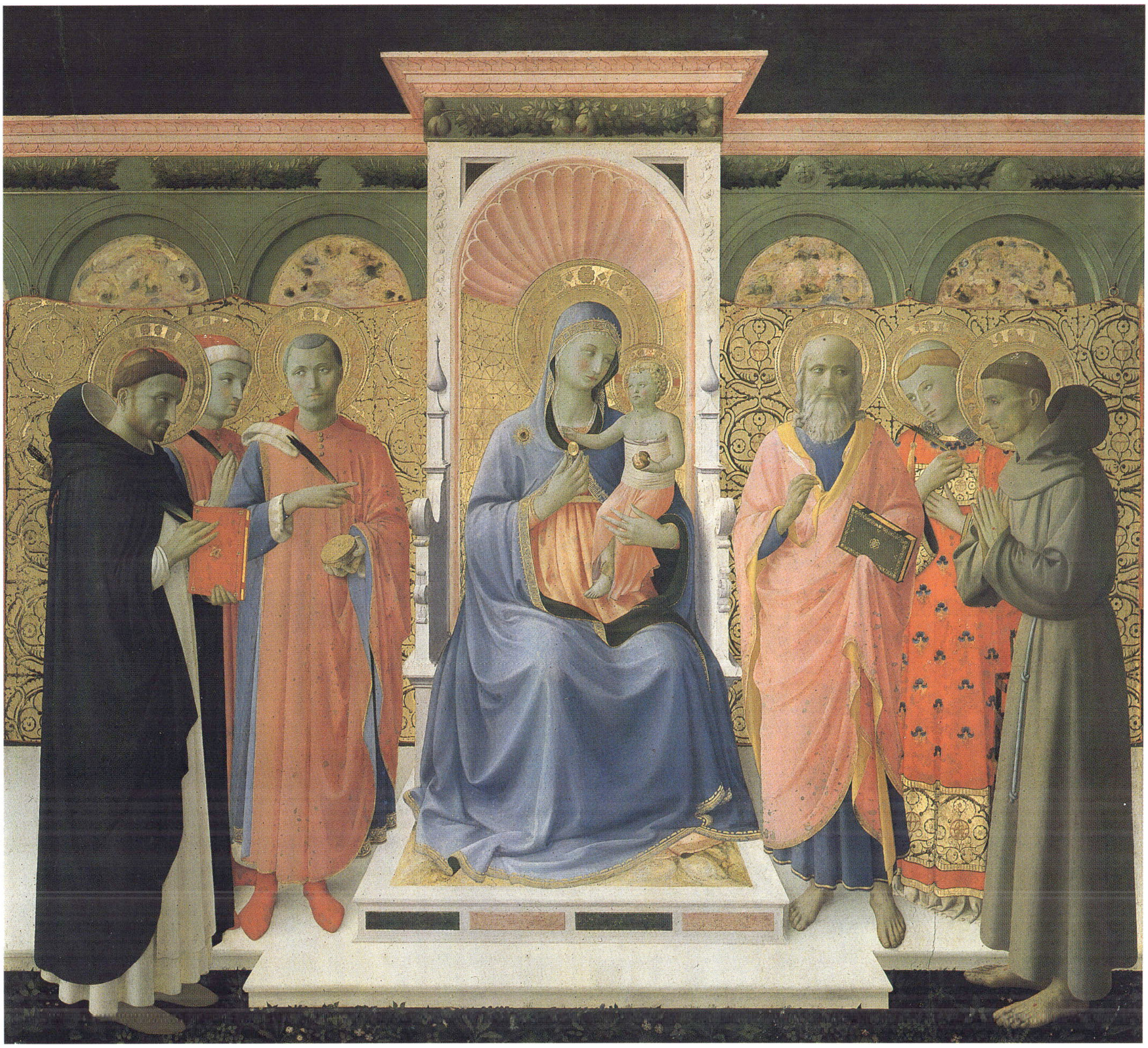

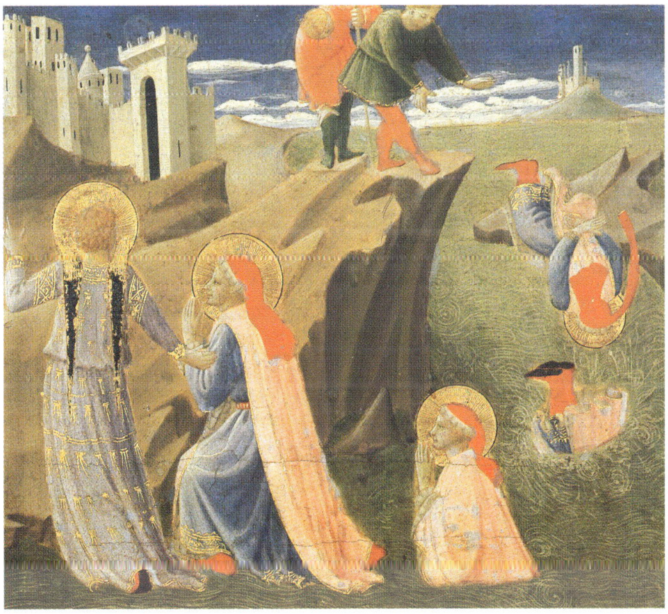

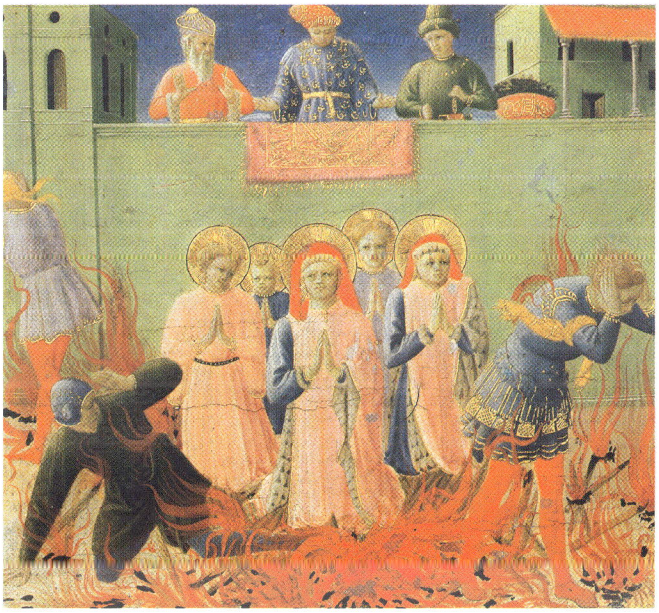

SAN MARCO ALTARPIECE

Having decided to renovate and embellish the main chapel of the church of San Marco, in late 1438 Cosimo the Elder donated the old altarpiece to the Dominican monastery of Cortona and replaced it with a new one worthy of the magnificence of the restored church. In the altarpiece a strict perspective scheme confers unity on the scene even amid a multitude of ornamental details, precious but significant words of a symbolic vocabulary. Kneeling before the enthroned Virgin, Cosmas and Damian, guardian saints of the Medici family, recall the patron of the work, creating, through the play of their positions, a relationship between the spectator and the painting. Emerging from this new figurative freedom and from the relationship between the personages portrayed is a singular equilibrium and a new dramatic sense of the sacred image, characteristics which make this work fully Renaissance in style. The choice of the saints appears rich in meaning; while the presence of Cosmas and Damian, Lawrence and John the Evangelist allude to the prominent family of the patron and to the city of Florence, Mark is the saint for whom the monastery and the church are named, while Francis, Peter and Dominic clearly allude to monastic piety. Festoons of roses symbolically recall the Virgin celebrated in the altarpiece, whose throne presents an architectural structure in the manner of Michelozzo, a translation into painting of the architectural style of the church of San Marco.

An icon portraying *Christ on the Cross* recalls the Passion of that same Child who appears in his mother's arms bestowing blessings.

The refined description of the embroidery on St Lawrence's dalmatic and his bejeweled pectoral testifies to Fra Angelico's assimilation of the lesson taught by Flemish painting, as well as to his seductive ability to describe reality with sharp insight. Flemish influence may be seen again in the magnificent Turkish carpet appearing in the foreground to demonstrate the painter's mastery of perspective.

The altarpiece was originally completed by a predella with the stories of Sts Cosmas and Damian (shown here *The Saints before Lysia* and *Christ dead with the Virgin and Saints*, now in Munich, Alte Pinakothek), distributed among various museums (Florence, San Marco Museum; Munich, Alte Pinakothek; Paris, The Louvre; Dublin, The National Gallery of Ireland; Washington, National Gallery of Art).

***San Marco Altarpiece* (*Madonna with Child, Angels and the Saints Cosmas and Damian, Lawrence, John the Evangelist, Mark, Dominic, Francis, Peter the Martyr*)**
tempera and gold on wood
220 x 227 (main panel), various sizes for each section of the predella; 1440-1442
Florence, San Marco Museum

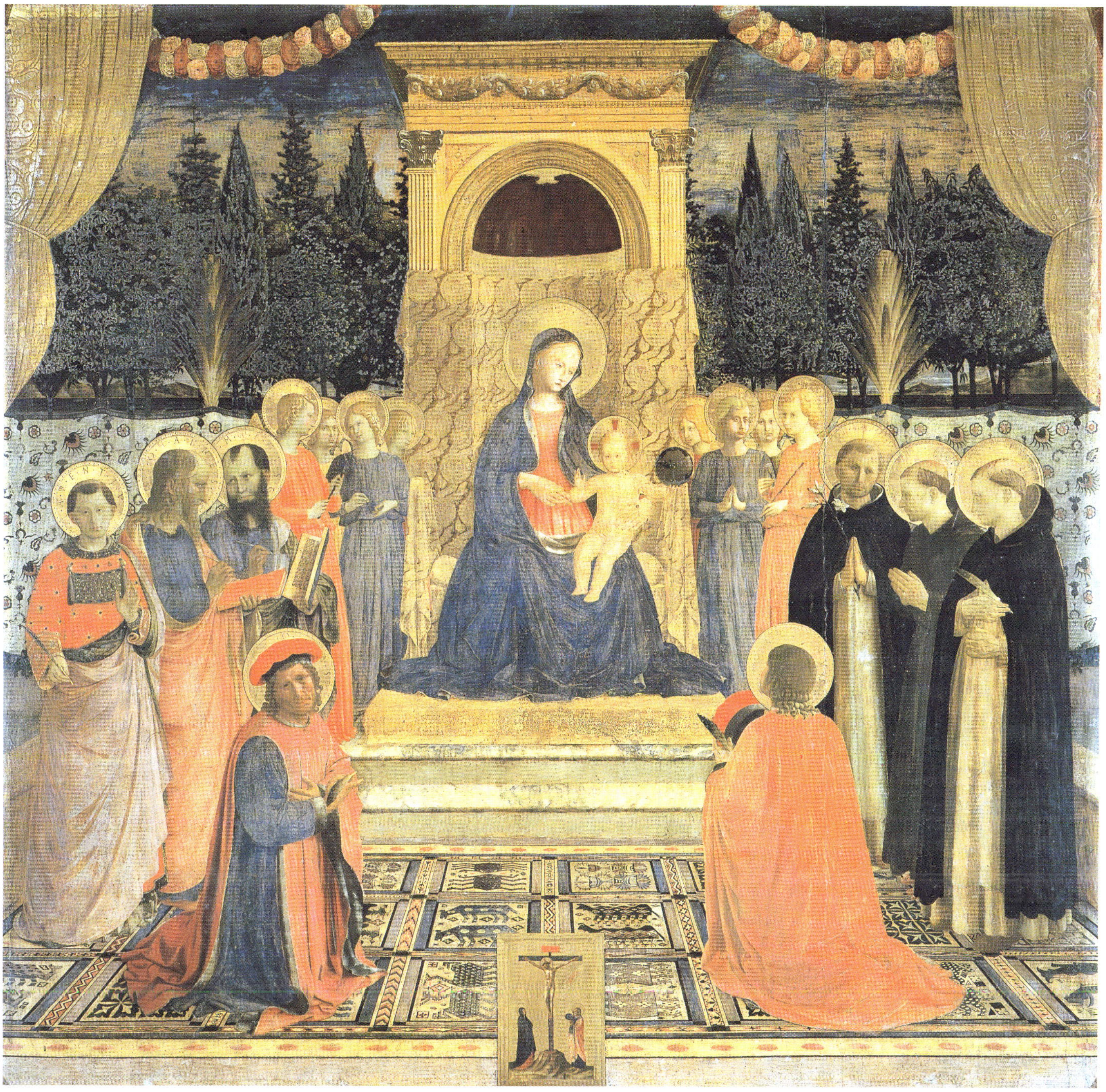

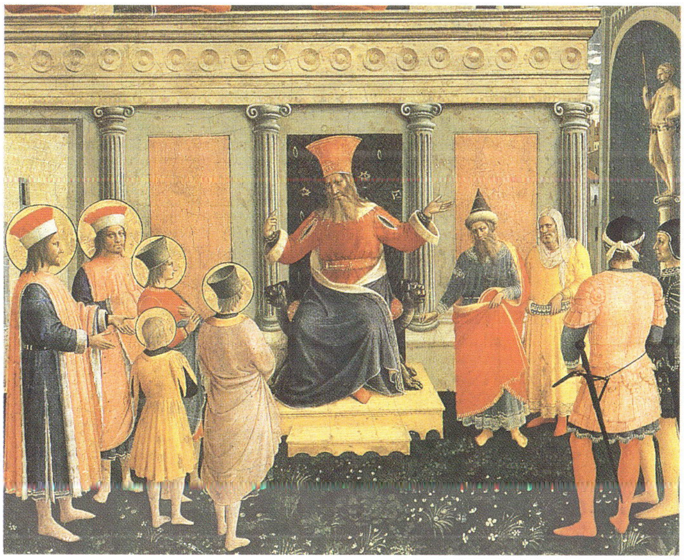

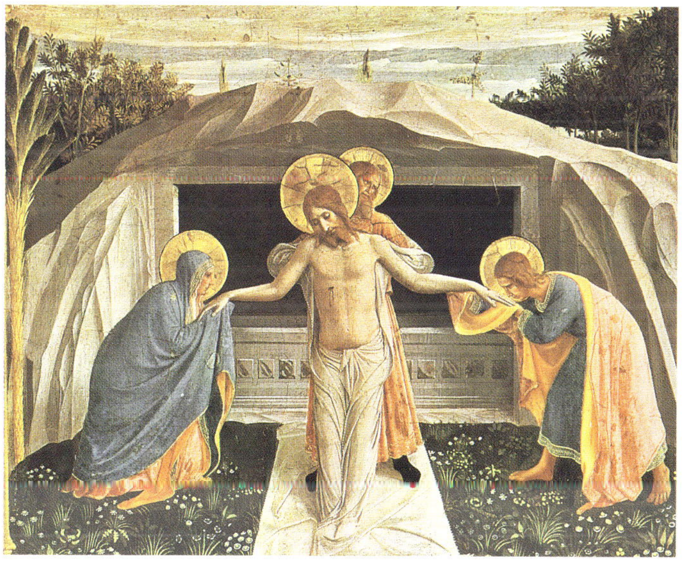

ADORATION OF THE MAGI

This fresco decorated cell 39, the one where Pope Eugene IV was housed on the occasion of the reconsecration of the monastery and the church, on the day of the Epiphany in 1443. The humanist Pope had been for some time in Florence, where he had been called to preside, in 1439, over the work of the "Council of Greeks". Numerous philosophers and personages from the Eastern Church had come to Florence to participate in the event, whose objective was the reunification of the Latin and the Greek churches. Still resounding in the fresco of the *Adoration* are echoes of what was designed to be the official encounter of two cultures, especially in the figures of the Wise Men from the East, the Magi, who bear their precious gifts to the newborn Christ, founder of Christianity and emblem of Occidental religiosity. Attention to precious, exotic details make this fresco a work very different in tone from the decoration of the other monastery cells. This has suggested that a good part of the fresco may be attributed to the hand of Benozzo Gozzoli, at that time still young but already the expert assistant of Fra Angelico. One of the reasons that make cell 39 particularly interesting is the fact that it was the personal cell of Cosimo the Elder. In fact, as thanks for the enormous amount of money he had contributed toward the restoration of the monastery Cosimo was granted the privilege, a highly unusual one, of using this double cell as a private retreat. The subject portrayed was almost an emblem for Cosimo, and was to be so for his successors as well.

Already by 1436 he had assumed control of the monastery and with it the Compagnia dei Magi headquartered there. This was a secular brotherhood which each year, on the occasion of the Epiphany, organized a splendid procession in commemoration of the Oriental kings, arriving at Bethlehem to worship the divine Child. Through the skillful and symbolic use of light, Fra Angelico describes the progressive enlightenment of the Three Kings as they approach Christ.

The armillary sphere borne by one of the Magi, symbol of the cosmos, may allude to the widespread idea among 15th century men of learning that the mysterious Oriental priests were above all expert astrologers, and as such capable of finding in the comet's celestial trajectory the route to be followed to arrive at the encounter with Christ.

Adoration of the Magi
fresco
175 x 357; 1438-1443
Florence, San Marco Museum, cell 39

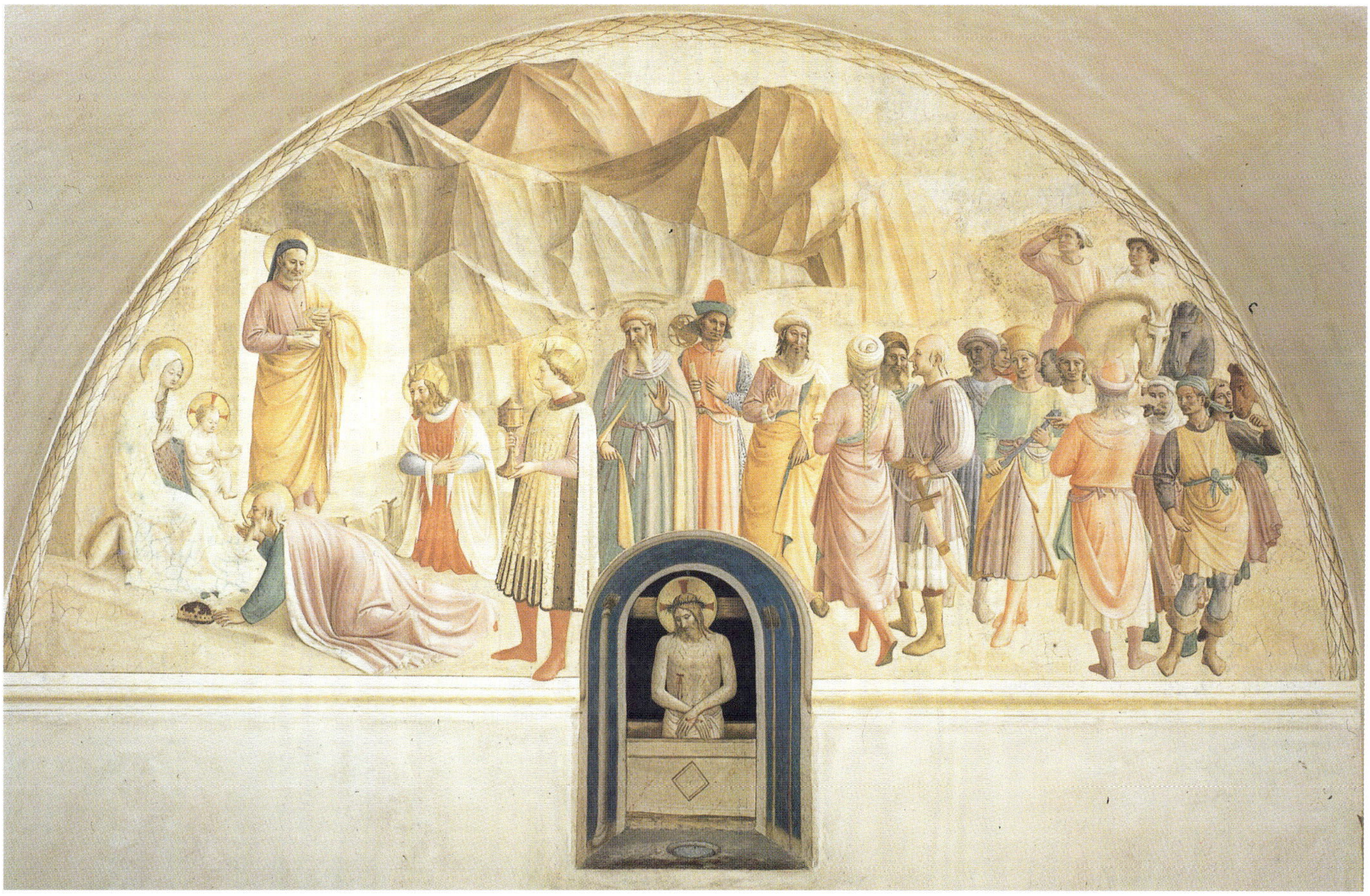

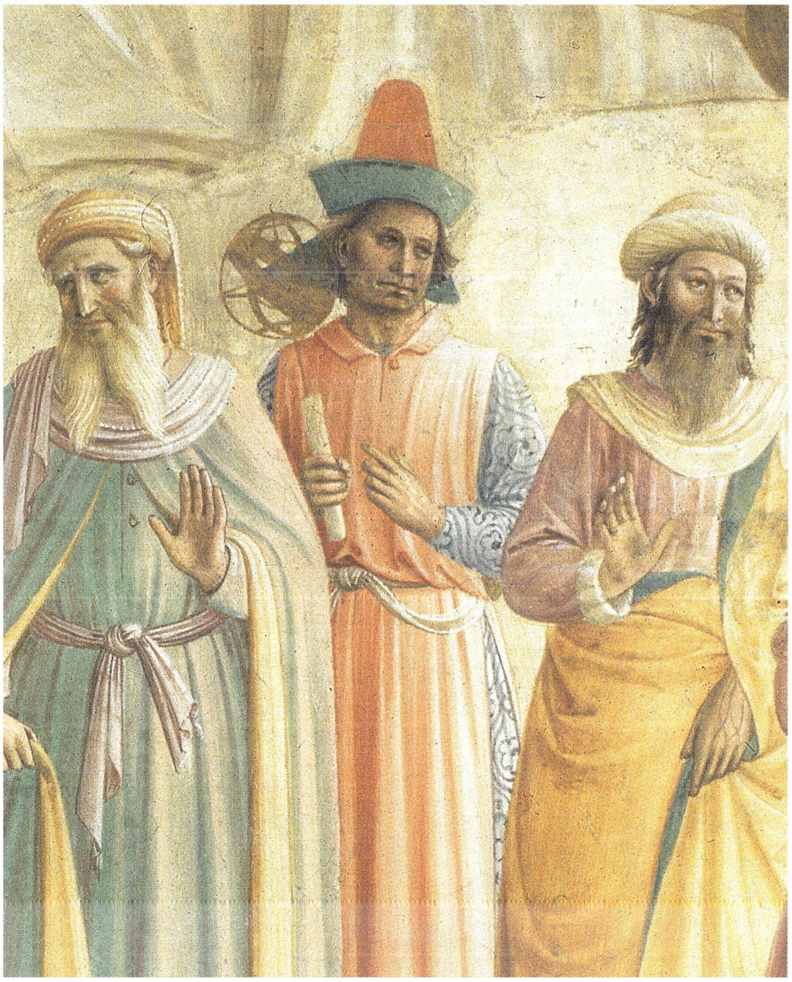

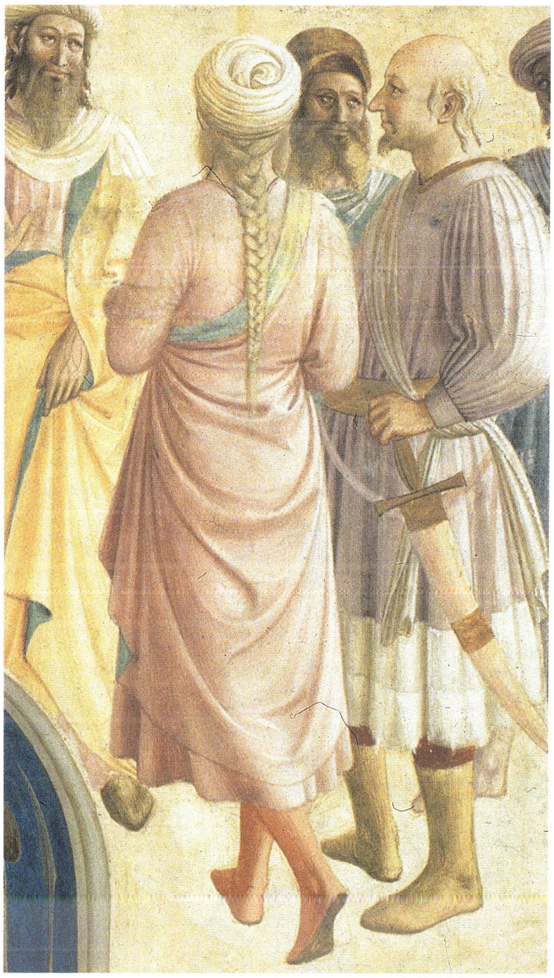

ORDINATION OF ST LAWRENCE

The *Ordination of St Lawrence* occupies the center of the wall between two windows. The scene is set in an imposing basilica, where the figures occupy the end of a cross-vaulted nave. A very close relationship exists between the architectural setting and the eight personages, identified through the detailed description of their liturgical gowns and an intense research in physiognomy. Two cardinals appear in their robes trimmed with gem-studded golden borders, two deacons wearing blue dalmatics – one of whom carries a copy of the New Testament – and three acolytes in white cottas, bearing censers and incense-boats. In the face of St Sixtus II have been recognized the features of Nicholas V, the great patron of the cycle of frescoes. The motif of the golden flames on St Lawrence's dalmatic recalls the martyrdom of the saint, condemned to be roasted alive on a grate, but also symbolizes the spirit of charity, since fire is symbolic of that virtue. The deacon holding a book, an attribute of St Lawrence, the patron saint of booksellers, calls attention to an interesting aspect of the personality of Nicholas V, a humanist and bibliophile. The Pope was in fact particularly generous with the scribes who ensured the survival of the ancient texts. The presence of the book also evokes the Pope's munificent acquisition of numerous volumes for the Vatican Library and, in general, his patronage of the Humanists, with whom he loved to surround himself. Among the most elegant details of the basilical architecture are the Corinthian capitals on the columns, which present a singular decoration with calla lilies embellishing the upper part of the capital and two rows of pomegranates in the middle. This is a refined citation of the columns in the portico of Solomon's temple demonstrating, once again, the erudition that pervades the work of Fra Angelico.

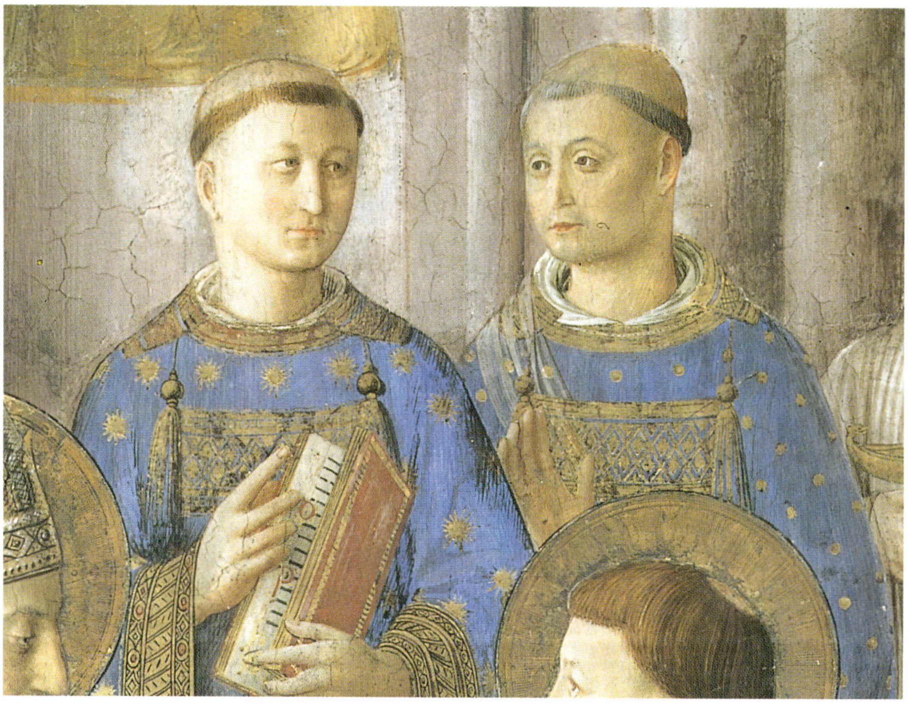

Ordination of St Lawrence
fresco
271 x 197; 1448
Vatican City, Vatican Palaces, Niccolina Chapel

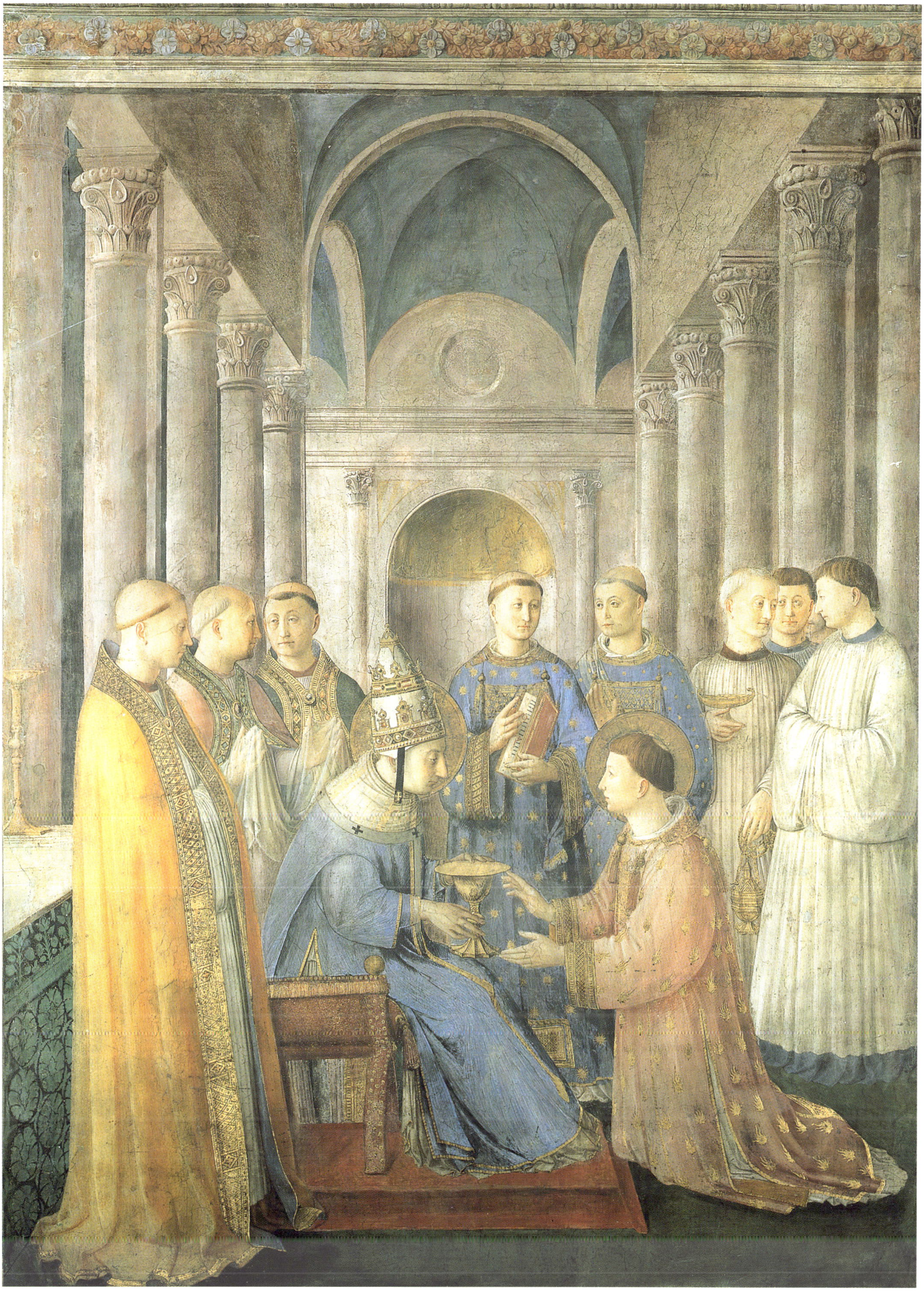

Index of names and works

Numbers in italic refer to illustrations and their captions.

Bibliography

Sources: L.B. Alberti, *Della pittura* (Florence, 1435-1436), edited by C. Grayson, Bari 1975; L. Ghiberti, *Commentari* (Florence, c. 1450-1455), ed. by J. von Schlosser, Berlin 1912; B. Facio, *De viris illustribus* (1453-1457), in M. Baxandall, *Giotto and the Orators*, Oxford 1971; Vespasiano da Bisticci, *Vite di uomini illustri del sec. XV* (c. 1480-1490), ed. by P. D'Ancona and E. Aeschlimann, Milan 1951; *Il Libro di Antonio Billi* (c. 1481-1536/1537), ed. by C. Frey, Berlin 1892; A. Manetti, *Uomini singolari in Firenze dal MCCCC innanzi* (c. 1482-1488), in *Operette istoriche edite ed inedite*, ed. by G. Milanesi, Florence 1887; F. Albertini, *Memoriale di molte statue et picture sono nella inclyta cipta di Florentia* (Florence 1510), Florence 1863; *Il Codice Magliabechiano* (c. 1537-1542), ed. by C. Frey, Berlin 1892 (new edition ed. by A. Ficarra, Naples 1968); G. Vasari, *Le vite de' più eccellenti pittori, scultori e architetti* (Florence 1568), ed. by G. Milanesi, Florence 1878-1885 (*The Lives of the Artists*, translated with an introduction and notes by J. Conaway Bondanella and P. Bondanella, Oxford University Press 1991); R. Borghini, *Il Riposo*, Florence 1584; F. Bocchi, G. Cinelli, *Le bellezze della città di Firenze*, Florence 1677; F. Baldinucci, *Notizie dei professori del disegno da Cimabue in qua...* (Florence 1681), ed. by F. Ranalli, Florence 1845-1847, reprinted with notes and index by P. Barocchi, A. Boschetto, Florence 1974, I, pp. 414-423; G. Richa, *Notizie istoriche delle chiese fiorentine*, I-X, Florence 1754-1762; L. Lanzi, *Storia pittorica della Italia inferiore*, Florence 1792; V. Marchese, *Memorie dei più insigni pittori, scultori e architetti domenicani*, Florence 1845, I; V. Marchese, *San Marco, Convento dei Padri Predicatori in Firenze, illustrato e inciso principalmente nei dipinti del B. Giovanni Angelico, con la vita dello stesso pittore e un sunto storico del Convento medesimo*, Florence 1851-1853; *La Cronaca del convento fiorentino di San Marco: la parte più antica, dettata da Giuliano Lapaccini*, ed. by R. Morçay, in «Archivio Storico Italiano», LXXI, 1913.

Critical literature: For reconstruction of the artist's life and works from the archives, see A. Serafini, *L'epopea cristiana nei dipinti del Beato Angelico. Nuovi studi e nuovi documenti*, Orvieto 1911; S. Orlandi, *Beato Angelico. Monografia storica della vita e delle opere*, Florence 1964; *Beato Angelico: miscellanea di studi*, ed. by the Postulazione Generale dei Domenicani, Rome 1984.

Monographs: J.A. Crowe, G.B. Cavalcaselle, *A History of Painting in Italy*, London 1864, II; R.L. Douglas, *Fra Angelico*, London 1900; A. Venturi, *Storia dell'arte italiana*, VII/1, Milan 1911; P. Muratoff, *Fra Angelico*, London-New York 1930; J. Pope-Hennessy, *Fra Angelico*, London 1952; G.C. Argan, *Fra Angelico*, Genève 1955; M. Salmi, *Il Beato Angelico*, Spoleto 1958; C. Urbani, *s.v.* in *Enciclopedia Universale dell'Arte*, Venice-Rome 1959; M. Levi D'Ancona, *Miniatura e miniatori a Firenze dal XIV al XVI secolo*, Florence 1962; D. Redig De Campos, *I Palazzi Vaticani*, Bologna 1967; L. Berti, *Angelico*, Florence 1967; U. Baldini, *L'opera completa dell'Angelico*, Milan 1970; J. Pope-Hennessy, *Fra Angelico*, London 1974; A. Greco, *La cappella di Niccolò V del Beato Angelico*, Rome 1980; T.S. Centi O.P., *Il Beato Giovanni Pittore Angelico*, Siena 1984; A. Garzelli, *Miniatura fiorentina del Rinascimento 1440 1525. Un primo censimento*, Florence 1985, I; U. Baldini, *Beato Angelico*, Florence 1986; L. Castelfranchi Vegas, *L'Angelico e l'Umanesimo*, Milan 1989; M.C. Improta, *La pittura su tavola dell'Angelico e del Quattrocento*, in *La chiesa e il convento di San Marco a Firenze*, II, Florence 1990; G. Bonsanti, *Gli affreschi del Beato Angelico*, ivi; A.M. De Strobel, F. Mancinelli, *Le camere "secrete": anticamera, cubicolo e cappella*, in *Raffaello nell'appartamento di Giulio II e Leone X*, Milan 1993; W. Hood, *Angelico at San Marco*, New Haven-London 1993; M. Levi D'Ancona, *The Illuminators and Illuminations of the Choir Books from Santa Maria Nuova in Florence*, Florence 1994; P. Morachiello, *Gli affreschi di San Marco*, Milan 1995; W. Hood, *Beato Angelico. Il Convento di San Marco a Firenze*, Turin 1995; *Gli affreschi del Beato Angelico nel Convento di San Marco*, ed. by D. Din, Turin 1996; J.T. Spike, *Angelico*, Milan 1996; G. Bonsanti, *Beato Angelico. Catalogo completo*, Florence 1998; C. Brandon Strehlke, *Angelico*, Milan 1998; M. Scudieri, *Museum of San Marco*, Florence 1999, G. Bonsanti, P. Morachiello, *Beato Angelico. Gli affreschi di San Marco*, Milan 2000; G. Cornini, *Beato Angelico*, Florence 2000; *Il Beato Angelico e la cappella Niccolina. Storia e restauro*, ed. by F. Buranelli, Novara 2001.

Catalogues: *Mostra delle opere del Beato Angelico nel quinto centenario della morte*, Vatican City 1955; *Mostra di arte sacra antica*, Florence 1961, with articles by L. Berti; G. Bonsanti, in *La città degli Uffizi*, Florence 1982; *L'età di Masaccio. Il primo Quattrocento a Firenze* (Florence 1990), ed. by L. Berti and A. Paolucci, Milan 1990; *Pittura di luce. Giovanni di Francesco e l'arte fiorentina di metà Quattrocento* (Florence 1990), ed. by L. Bellosi with articles by L A. De Marchi, Milan 1990; *Una scuola per Piero. Luce, colore, prospettiva nella formazione fiorentina di Piero della Francesca* (Florence, 1992-1993), ed. by L. Bellosi, Venice 1992; C. Syre, *Die Münchner Tafeln und der Hochaltar von San Marco in Florenz*, Munich 1996; *Beato Angelico e Benozzo Gozzoli. Artisti del Rinascimento a Perugia* (Perugia 1999), ed. by V. Garibaldi, Cinisello Balsamo 1998; *Masaccio e le origini del Rinascimento* (San Giovanni Valdarno 2002-2003), ed. by L. Bellosi with the collaboration of L. Cavazzini and A. Galli, Milan 2002.

Photographic acknowledgements

All the photographs are from the Giunti Archive, except: 15b (Giunti Archive/Photo Stefano Giraldi); 20, 25 (Giunti Archive/Photo Nicola Grifoni); cover, 4b, 6-7, 12a, 13, 16, 18,19, 22, 23, 24, 31, 32a, 33, 35a, 36b-c, 38, 43, 44, 45, 50, 51, 53a-b, 57a (Giunti Archive/Photo Rabatti & Domingie); 55, 59 (Rabatti & Domingie Photography, Florence); 38-39, 41, 60, 61 (Photo Scala, Florence).
As concerns rights to reproduction, the publisher is willing to pay any amounts due for photographs for which it has been impossible to determine the source.